ROLLIN'

IN THE

DOUGH

ROLLIN'
IN THE
DOUGH

BY EVANGELINE MARONITIS RIEGLER

TATE PUBLISHING
AND ENTERPRISES, LLC

Published by Tate Publishing & Enterprises, LLC
127 E. Trade Center Terrace | Mustang, Oklahoma 73064 USA
1.888.361.9473 | www.tatepublishing.com

Tate Publishing is committed to excellence in the publishing industry. The company reflects the philosophy established by the founders, based on Psalm 68:11,
"The Lord gave the word and great was the company of those who published it."

Book design copyright © 2015 by Tate Publishing, LLC. All rights reserved.
Cover design by Nikolai Purpura
Interior design by Jake Muelle

Published in the United States of America

ISBN: 978-1-68028-328-0
1. Business & Economics / Home-Based Businesses
2. Cooking / Courses & Dishes / Pastry
15.09.18

This book is dedicated to the three most important men that have been in my life.

First to my father, who taught me the very essence of perseverance and hard work coupled with honor to your country, church, and family equaled a successful life not measured in dollars and cents.

Secondly, to my dear son, who put up with me during his preteen and teenage years as I pursued my dream of owning my own business.

Third, to my husband, who dedicated himself to helping me the last two years of my ownership of my business. He has been trying to do everything possible since then to help me with any endeavors I have wanted to pursue.

This book is also dedicated to my mother, who taught me the joy of baking. She and I always loved to purchase cookie recipe books and eagerly anticipated tasting these new recipes. When I have taught children how to measure ingredients, I tell them that leveling off is the way my mother taught me and this is the proper way to do it.

Without the love, support and guidance from all of them, I could have never conceived nor dreamt my ideas into the reality of owning my business.

Contents

Introduction

This story has been written for those who want to turn their dream into their successful business. Despite financial obstacles and family and friends who do not give the emotional support that you may need, know that faith in yourself will help you fulfill your dreams. Do not be afraid to try. Many well-known personalities throughout history have stated that if you fail, just try again. It is true that certain failures can produce success. It is called a learning experience.

Just imagine now that you are sitting in the living room of my shop, and we are drinking a cup of coffee. You have asked me just how it all began. So if you're a coffee drinker, pour yourself a cup of coffee now, get comfortable in your chair, and let me tell you the way it all happened.

1

Greeks Love a Lamb,
but Not a Black Sheep

There I was, forty years old. The writing was on the wall—or rather, the etching was on the glass ceiling in my banking job. It would be pretentious to call what I had a career, although in today's World of McJobs, perhaps it was. I just considered myself a single working mom. The only work I really knew was banking or restaurant work.

In high school, I took the college prep courses because I wanted to be a teacher. I loved children, and my father always stressed to me that if I taught school, I would have my summers off so that I could be with my children. My mother had never really spent any summers with me when I was growing up, except when I was a baby and toddler, naturally.

I started working the summer I was fourteen at my parent's restaurant. I loved it there. At first, I was only allowed to be a bus girl and put away clean dishes. Eventually I was shown how to work the soda fountain. The waitresses appreciated the help I was giving them.

I especially loved to go into the kitchen and watch my father. All of his cooking was homemade, and he rejected all shortcuts. His food sales representatives would pitch to him about the innovative new frozen French fries and instant mashed potatoes. Not for my father! The very thought of those things made him upset.

My father never seemed to stop. I used to sit on a stool in his restaurant kitchen and watch him work. Sometimes he would talk to me, but mostly he concentrated on what he was doing, which was a good thing. I knew not to interrupt him with any childlike chatter. Not that Pop would be angry; I just didn't want to disturb him. I could see he was concentrating on his work.

He cut all of his own meats. The most fun though was watching him push down the chunks of red meat into his food grinder and seeing it come out as ground meat. Pop would grab a precise portion of this meat and form each ball into a hamburger patty. Talk about good eye; he didn't use an ice cream scoop. He placed layers of waxed sheets between the patties as he laid them into a large pan. When the pan was filled, he would cover it and place it into the refrigerator. He just kept going all day long, taking care of job after job in his beloved kitchen.

Sometimes, after the completion of his task, he would say, "Huoney bunch, I sure could use *enna* cups coffee." That meant he wanted one cup of coffee. I always replied, "I'll go get it for you, Pop," because this gave me a chance to do something for him. It also gave me the opportunity to check out what was going on in the dining room. I wasn't allowed in there so that I would not get in anyone's way... especially Mother's.

Cheerfully, I would return to the kitchen and carefully place the cup and saucer next to Pop's work area. He would always say, "You know, honeybunch, you the only one that

ever goes to get me *enna* cups coffee or a *Goga Kollo* (Coke)."
This pronunciation was his Greek humor, and I will not tell
you what this means translated into American. For those of
you who know Greek, smile.

More often than not, I would hear my Pop humming
as he worked but did not realize at the time the melodies
he hummed. I especially did not know that the music he
had in his memories was the driving force that got him
through his long hours at his restaurant, which he dearly
loved almost as much as his wife and children. As the Bible
says in Ephesians 5:19, "Sing and make music in your head
to the Lord."

In my preteen years, I didn't realize that Pop kept up his
hectic pace because he plied himself with black coffee or a
Coke. The caffeine he was taking in enabled him to keep
going during his twelve to fourteen hours, six days a week
in the restaurant. He never lost his cool. He just kept going.

Years later, it dawned on me. Yes, he was caffeinated to
the hilt, just as I was doing the same thing. But I smiled at
Pop's little secret: his love of his church's music and, most
of all, God are what kept him going, not the coffee or coke
as I thought.

Initially, when Mom and Pop opened their last restaurant, they were open on Sundays, but after establishing their new place, they were able to have Sundays away
from their daily routine. Being closed on Sundays was a big
deal to my siblings when they owned their places of business. Six days really is enough, and yes, Sunday should be
reserved for God.

When school began, I worked after school each night
until closing at 9:00 p.m. and then went home with either
Pop or my brother. Hours of homework waited for me. I

gave it my all until 11:00 p.m. and made my mom promise to wake me up at 5:00 a.m. so that I could complete my studies. I've always been an early bird.

By the time I graduated from high school, I had saved $2,000, which I thought was a lot of money. I soon found out that this fortune I had accumulated fell a bit short the cost of four years of college. So after almost two years of scrimping and struggling with finances at college, I had to take a break from school and find a job.

I could have returned to the restaurant, but I wanted to try something different. My father didn't indicate his disappointment, but I knew he felt really bad for me that I was not in college. At that particular time, they were not able to help me with my expenses.

In my high school, if you didn't take bookkeeping or shorthand and typing, you were enrolled in college prep courses. A simple enough plan, but if you could no longer go to college, what the heck were you prepared to do?

A lady at my church worked as a teller at the bank where my parents did business, and I always thought that could be a good job. The more I thought about it, the better the idea seemed to me. So I got on the bus and went downtown to the bank. I didn't have an appointment and had never heard of a personnel department, so I just asked at the teller's window who to see about a job.

In my interview, I told the personnel manager that I knew how to wait on customers and could run a cash register. It didn't hurt that his wife was Greek. He must have figured that since my heritage was Greek and had grown up in a family restaurant, I was probably a hard worker. I was. I was also raised to understand customer service although that term was not in our vocabulary. We just knew that the people who came into our business needed to be taken care of properly.

I was hired on the spot as a teller. Through the years, I advanced through several various departments until I became operations supervisor in the commercial loan department at another bank.

I was a woman without a degree. In those days, that meant that no matter how efficiently I ran any department, my grade level was not going to change. Therefore I could not advance, and there would be no chance to increase my wages. Besides, I was forty.

My mom was always a working mother, and I didn't like it at all. Coming home to an empty house was depressing. This was before the term *latchkey* came into being, but I guess I was a latchkey kid.

My childhood had lots of lonely moments because of the long hours my parents worked. The upside is that those times gave me the freedom to think and imagine and dream.

It may seem strange, but my most exhilarating times were when I was swept up by the rapture of planning the future and dreaming while I was sitting under the huge maple tree in our yard or weeding my father's garden for him. So many of these me times were filled with this strange inner feeling that someday I would have a restaurant or bakery in some kind of older home. It would be small, but not too small. It would be a house that I really loved, and it would have a shop that no one else had nor had even conceived. It would be a gathering place.

I had two sisters, one older, one younger and both of them were married to very successful business owners. Of course, their husbands were Greek, and my sisters worked side by side with them. My older brother married a nice Greek girl who also worked diligently by his side in their restaurant.

I was the black sheep. I didn't marry a Greek and was divorced. I didn't have my own business and certainly didn't enjoy the affluence that the rest of my family had obtained.

The move that I was contemplating would be very upsetting to my mother. Secretly, I knew my Pop would understand. But the perception with the majority of my family would definitely be "Who does she think she is?"

I was going against my Greek heritage by daring to start a business as a divorcee instead of getting remarried and helping my spouse with his business. Plus, I would be leaving a perfectly good job at a bank with a regular paycheck, and I had a child to support. So I kept my dreams and aspirations all to myself.

2

When You Learn to Swim,
You Have to Jump in the Deep End

I didn't go to my brother's restaurant often, but every time I drove there, my eyes were drawn to the cute Dutch colonial house catty-cornered from his place. It was occupied by a nursery school, but the yard was unkempt. Over time, I noticed that the yard was terribly overgrown; the business sign in the front yard was down. The place looked vacant.

I started paying more attention to the house. One day I noticed something that took my breath away. There was a For Sale sign in the yard.

In a flash, I went through the deepest session of soul-searching I had ever experienced. I was excited, committed, eager, and cautious all at the same time. What I was *not* was afraid. I just loved this house. Something told me this was my opportunity, and it was the right thing to do.

First, I needed to sell my current home. That was extremely difficult. I could write a small book on the experience, but I'm not very fond of horror stories, especially when I'm the main character. I have plenty of drama to communicate in the acquisition of my cute Dutch colonial.

This house had a converted apartment on the second floor and retail space on the first floor. That arrangement was ideal for my plan. The frosting on this cookie was that it was zoned commercial.

I had no experience as a business owner, but I grew up surrounded by family-owned businesses. What I did know was commercial loans and financing of business real estate. It would take every ounce of my accumulated knowledge and skill as a banker to secure the financing on this property.

I promptly started out by making a big mistake. I called the name indicated on the yard sign instead of getting another realtor to be my buyer's agent. The agent on the sign is trying to sell the house. That agent is allowed to also represent you as you buy it, but serving two masters is rarely beneficial to either master. Oh well, live and learn.

I worked up the courage to go see my boss to ask for a commercial loan to purchase the cute little Dutch colonial on the corner of Sixth and North Main Street in North Canton. I told him that I was selling my current residence and planned to use those proceeds to renovate the new property.

I was totally unprepared for his reaction. He flat out denied me my loan request. He based his denial on his reluctance to be the one that would have to evict me if I didn't succeed. Gee, what a swell excuse!

Undaunted, I called three other of my buddies at the other banks downtown. I knew these guys, and they knew me. I had a reputation for being a very knowledgeable and hard-working person.

I gave them my proposal, but they all turned me down and gave the same excuse. I was told that I was their friend and that they could never throw me out onto the street. I was so depressed.

My sister had given me some restaurant trade magazines, and that evening, I skimmed through them. I always liked to look at them to get ideas. One of the magazines had a wonderful story about a woman who had grown up in the Carolinas, where she learned to make really good barbecue. Her dream had always been to open a barbecue restaurant. So after she had settled into her new home, in San Francisco, she gathered up her plans and went to her new bank. She was flatly denied a loan to fund her dream venture because after all, San Francisco is known as the city of restaurants. All the bankers told her that another restaurant in their city was not needed. The bankers' denial after denial certainly sounded familiar—perhaps a different reason, but a denial nonetheless. How I felt her pain. I kept reading her story. This lady was quite persistent. She proceeded to go to twenty-four more banks. And finally, the twenty-fourth bank granted her a loan. She turned into one of those dream stories. She took in a million dollars her first year. You see, she didn't have any competition and her place was completely unique.

I couldn't believe my good luck. I had already talked to four banks and just had to find twenty more!

The next morning, a very appreciative customer, Pat, called me at the bank and asked if she could take me to lunch. Her boss, Jim, a very successful and generous business owner, used to have her call me about once a month and treat me to lunch. It was his way of saying thanks for the great service he got from my department. I agreed to meet her.

At lunch, Pat could see that I had something on my mind. She asked what was up, and I just broke down and told her about my ideas and my ultimate rejection from my supposed friends. I swore her to secrecy. She was really upset with the attitude that these male bankers had given me.

She promised that she would talk to Jim that afternoon and get the name of the new commercial loan officer up in Akron that he had been talking to in regard to moving his accounts to another bank.

I promised Pat that I would not let my boss know about Jim's intention to move his accounts. I really appreciated Jim talking to his new potential commercial loan officer about me. It was unheard of if you lived in Canton, Ohio, and had your business in Canton, Ohio, for you to deal with an Akron bank or any other out-of-town bank.

After lunch, she called me with his name and phone number. She also told me that Jim had already called him to pave the way for my phone call. His name was Bob, and he agreed to meet me the very next day.

I knew how these guys operated and decided to use that knowledge to my benefit. When he told me where his favorite new place was, I was overjoyed. God was watching over me. The owners were long-time Greek friends of mine. I met Bob at their place and ran a tab. Bob loved Beck's beer, so I made sure Smiley, the bar manager, kept Bob's glass filled with his favorite.

Bob wrote down a rate on a cocktail napkin and passed it over to me. I sweetly smiled and put a line through his number. I wrote my rate on the napkin and passed it back to him. Bob read it and grinned as he said, "Okay, you talked me into it." I nearly went into shock. I had my loan and at a rate I did not deserve.

I was an inexperienced business owner, and I knew that the highest risk businesses were in the food industry. I never thought for a moment that he would agree to my ridiculous offer. But he did because I had the nerve and conviction to ask for it. Someone that didn't know me not only granted me my loan but also at the rate and terms I requested.

I think Bob must have peeked in the windows of my little house before we met because he said, "You know, you're going to outgrow this place in a year."

I quickly told him, "Bob, I just want to be in business in a year."

Bob then said, "Oh well, if you belly up, you can come up to Akron and run my department. I sure could use you."

I closed on my loan in less than thirty days and had my other house sold too. I had to get the remodeling done as quickly as possible, but I bumped into unexpected difficulties.

I was used to working with highly educated men all day long, and they always showed me great respect. All my customers at the bank were men as well, and I had a great working relationship with them.

My plumber and electrician were great, but it was another matter working with my remodeler. For one thing, he didn't seem to understand that I was writing the checks for the work. I wasn't some bimbo being humored with her sugar daddy's bankroll.

I admit, I have always been very opinionated, and I was fearful of cost overruns, which would very quickly deplete my working capital. This made me a demanding boss. Deal with it, buster.

I fired the first contractor and should have dumped the second one as well, but I was desperate to get everything done in a timely manner. I needed to get open. I was making payments and did not have a monthly income. Well,

I finally got open the second week of November without physically harming even one construction guy.

I had lots of curious seekers coming in every day. They became regulars, and so I entered my first Thanksgiving and Christmas season not knowing quite what to expect.

I knew I traded in my very roomy split-level in the suburbs for lots and lots of long hours filled with tiring work. My son and I now lived in three rooms on top of the shop.

I thought my twelve-year-old son could handle the hours that I needed to put into my new shop. What I will always regret is not anticipating that he was not me at his age. Sure, he was proud of his mom, but more often than not, he was very angry. And he didn't even know why. The recent changes in our lifestyle and the start of my new business collided with hormones and teenage rebellion. What a tough combination for a kid to have to deal with. So our years were often a struggle, but I felt so lucky to be there when he walked in from school. He didn't get it.

3

Oh God, What Have I Done?

I opened Evie's Emporium on a cold Monday in the second week of November in 1985. Don't bother to check the records books because it was not exactly a big deal. Only to me.

I had worked like a crazy lady the day before preparing cookie dough and was up bright and early baking cookies. At 7:30 a.m. I hung up the Open sign and waited. And waited. And waited some more. Finally, around nine o'clock, Nancy Blue walked in. I introduced myself and welcomed her.

It was always my policy to offer a free cookie to anyone on their first visit to my shop. I offered Nancy a free cookie, and she graciously accepted. Although she had a very trim shape, Nancy had an immense sweet tooth. She liked my policy, and she liked the cookie.

Nancy became a constant customer and made many referrals to my shop. She was curious about the new operation. Nancy had been following the progress of the remodeling and had made careful note of the signs I posted in my windows promising the impending official opening. Nancy knew nearly everyone in North Canton and had appointed herself as my official customer/historian.

Let me describe some of my other first customers. I will never forget everything they did for me and how fond I became of them.

The second curious seeker of my opening day was a Federal illegal, David the mailman. Let me explain. His mail route ended in my parking lot at the rear of my house. I was not a designated break stop for his route. But that didn't stop David from popping in every day.

He had grown up with a bunch of Greek kids and had been stationed in Greece during his tour in the US Navy. He had heard a single Greek girl was opening a bakery and figured he'd find lots of Greek cookies. The fact that I never made Greek cookies, except for Greek butterball cookies at Christmas, never slowed him down from stopping in everyday.

David was semi-outraged that I did not make Greek cookies, and I had to explain the matter to him. Mom and I always made American cookies because mom's sister, Sophie, made fabulous Greek pastries. So we didn't. However, there were some American specialties that only Aunt Sophie made.

One of my first customers was a lady, active in North Canton society, who was known for having her way. One day she called me and inquired, "Do you make really good cornbread? I need some for my luncheon tomorrow. Can I pick it up in the morning?"

I immediately answered, "Yes, I do make excellent cornbread. I use my Aunt Sophie's recipe, and I'm sure you will like it very much." She did, and I know Aunt Sophie is smiling now because I am sharing her recipe with you.

I must tell you right now that I learned the hard way to always make sure you have all the necessary ingredients before you start preparing your recipe. I preached this rule to the employees I eventually had in my shop.

So here's Aunt Sophie's recipe. Make sure you have everything you need before you begin.

*   *   *

Aunt Sophie's Cornbread

Ingredients

1 1/2 cups cornmeal
1 cup flour
1/2 teaspoon salt
2 1/2 teaspoons baking powder
1/2 teaspoon baking soda
3/4 cup vegetable oil
2 eggs, beaten
1 3/4 cups of buttermilk
3/4 teaspoon vanilla
3/4 cup sugar

Preheat oven to 350 degrees. In a medium bowl, mix cornmeal, flour, salt, baking powder, baking soda, and sugar. In a large bowl, beat vegetable oil, eggs, buttermilk, and vanilla.

Gradually add dry ingredients to buttermilk mixture and mix until smooth. Pour into a well-greased 9 × 13 × 2 pan. Bake for 25–30 minutes until a toothpick inserted into the middle comes out clean.

Remove from oven and cool on wire cooling rack.

* * *

I have often wondered that if Aunt Sophie lived today and had the opportunity for a higher education, she would have been our first woman president. She was very organized and quite a hard worker. She headed many successful committees with her women's group at church. She was Mother's oldest sister and quite a fabulous cook and baker.

I always loved going to her house especially in the summertime so I could stroll through her beautiful vegetable and flower garden. My father had a great garden, but Aunt Sophie's was laid out differently.

Mother always looked up to her older sister because she respected her knowledge for so many things. I appreciated Aunt Sophie calling me every night as I lay in bed trying to go to sleep. She always asked how my day went. She never failed to tell me how proud she was of me. The affirmation of her pride and love in me encouraged me to go on as a businesswoman.

* * *

In those early days of my shop, I met Bernie Clements, the owner of the local newspaper. Bernie stopped in on a cold call seeking an ad. We immediately became friends. On this visit, he was trying to get me to place a coupon in a whole page of coupons he was trying to fill. I had never seriously thought of advertising in the North Canton Sun, plus I had no idea how effective coupons were. Bernie said some people will cash in on the coupon offer and never be seen again. Some will try the coupon offer and become steady customers. You can never tell, but a coupon would be a relatively minor expense, and it might produce some business.

I decided to give it a try. While Bernie had been talking with me about coupons, I had to brainstorm. Everyone knows that a baker's dozen is thirteen cookies for the price of twelve. I decided to have Bernie run a coupon for my shop offering an Evie's dozen. Since I wanted people to learn that my shop was *special*, the coupon would give the customer fourteen cookies for the price of twelve. Bernie said that might make the coupon stand out and generate some response, but there were no promises.

Bernie said he'd take care of creating the coupon for the ad. He wished me good luck and said he'd bill me after the promotion.

I was excited. The day the paper came out, I eagerly went through the pages until I came to the page of coupons. There was my coupon offering an Evie's dozen. I had baked extra cookies to meet the anticipated response.

I didn't need to bother. In the week that the coupon ran, *two* coupons were redeemed. I have no clue who brought them in. The coupon was not a moneymaker. But Bernie had been honest with me. I liked his style and his honesty. I had not made large cookie sales, but I had made a business friend. One that would be there for me many times as I struggled to make Evie's a success.

Bernie took a great interest in my shop, and often, when he needed to get away from his office, he would drop in for a cup of coffee. He knew my free coffee pot was always on for my friends. Sooner or later, the phone would ring, and the voice on the other end would ask, "Is he in there?" It was his wife, Gwynne, needing resolution to some print problem. I would laugh, and Bernie knew his impromptu break was over.

* * *

I have always been able to remember names and faces. It was easy for me to determine if someone had been into the shop before. But how I really was able to detect these first-time visitors was because they wore a little kid expression on their faces.

The shop smelled good. I baked off trays of cookies all day so that when they came in, the first remark they would make is "Oh, it smells so good in here." I would smile and secretly think, *You bet it does. I made sure of it.* The look of wonder was also a good clue that they had never been in before. A repeated response was "Why, it's like being at my grandmother's house." I smiled inside. That was the whole point.

I always greeted the new ones with a complimentary cookie and introduced myself. I always welcomed them to my home—not my business per se, but into my home because it was my home first, then my business.

Trying to instill this philosophy into my employees later on was not always easy. Sometimes, they just did not understand the concept. But my customers sure did and they liked it!

My shop was not the usual where you step into the room and there is a glass showcase of baked goods. My guests had to walk into the living room. I had chosen a wallpaper design from the Cookie Jar collection. It was a light-cream background with pin stripes of wheat and small little light burgundy rose buds in between the stripes. My windows had ruffled curtains, like the kind I had grown up with. I had my grandmother's dining room set in the living room. My mother loved colonial furniture, and so did I.

I am happy to say that Mother was coming around to the idea of my shop. Sometimes, she would call with her suggestion of recipes for some of the cookies she thought I should offer in the shop.

Mom was always right. She had an uncanny sense of business, and I saw this when she and Pop ran their restaurant. I learned to bend over backward to try to please my customers just as my parents had done in their restaurant. Again, this was something that I had to instill in my employees.

Shortly after I opened, Mom asked Stephen (my son) and me over for dinner. She surprised me by giving me her KitchenAid mixer. It was still in very good condition. Mom explained that she wanted a newer model. I was so excited. I have to tell you, I always felt that my mom was part witch. Talk about woman's intuition. Her instinct told her that I needed another mixer and could not afford to buy one. This is what she knew. I only had the very nice Hamilton Beach stainless mixer I had had for years, but it would not accommodate a double batch of cookie dough. Mom's KitchenAid sure could, and Mom figured I needed this additional mixer. She was so right.

It was a good sign that I needed another piece of equipment even though I didn't have the funds to purchase it. I must have been making progress. And so it was that I now had another mixer, which was the forerunner of many more KitchenAids that I would buy.

Over the years, I was often questioned, "Why don't you get a floor model?" First of all, I would not have had the strength to carry those big bowls around and most importantly; Grandma didn't have one of those in her kitchen, did she?

The concept of walking into the living room, being greeted with hospitality and the place smelling so good worked.

At my shop, when you bought a dozen cookies, your purchase was treated the same as if you had just picked up two hundred cookies. Buy six dozen or ten dozen, the care and attention to detail we gave those cookies was always the best.

I always placed a paper doily on a paper plate then arranged the cookie purchase such as a dozen frosted cut-outs. Then I pulled clear plastic wrap over the top and always offered a tie of ribbon and quick bow. I always made sure of this packaging just in case they were taking their cookies to someone as a gift.

The cookie sale was as much the heart of Evie's as any other item. We treated the cookie with care and respect. And we always treated our customers the same way. The old "just throw it in a box" did not go over with me.

Soon, my strategy caught on. Boxes were for cakes, not cookies, although sometimes, I did put them in a box if they were taking the cookies home or somewhere and they would be arranged with other cookies on a platter.

Platters. I soon realized that I arranged cookie platters much better than my customers did. They didn't have the expertise, and they didn't have the time, so I made them an unheard of offer. I told them if they brought me their platters, I would arrange their purchase for them. They were wild about this idea. Obviously, it saved them time. But the hidden benefit was that they could tell their guests that they had made the cookies, which they proudly displayed on their platters. They often confessed that is the scheme they had thought of all by themselves. My hidden benefit in this deception was that if my customer brought in her tray to be arranged, it saved me the cost of using my disposable ones. It was a win-win situation for both of us. I was always extremely careful to tag each platter with the buyer's name, order, date, and time of pick-up. I never had a mistake on this.

Only once was I really aggravated. Joycie, my first "full-time part-timer," nearly had a fit. A very prominent lady dropped off a large silver tray for her cookie order. That gorgeous platter had never been cleaned. I sent Joycie to the grocery store to get silver polish, and Joycie made that platter sparkle. We didn't charge extra, but we sure laughed about that one for years.

I suddenly realized that I needed to have arranged platters on display. The first one I did was a disposable one with a doily, arranged with three dozen assorted cookies. Customers came in, walked over to the platter, and said, "Oh, can I order this"?

Then it dawned on me. It was obvious that they were ordering what they saw, so why was I displaying a three-dozen platter? I promptly changed the display to a five-dozen platter with the increased price. Sure enough, my customers continued to order what they saw. I am shocked today that when I enter practically any type of store and am virtually ignored by the sales personnel until I have stepped up to the cash register with my money in my hand. Stores don't employ sales help anymore; they just have cashiers.

So many days when I was by myself, I would silently cry, *Oh God, what have I done?* There was always a bill to pay. I always paid cash for my groceries. My brother often said, "A $100 meat bill could turn into a $2000 meat bill. Always pay cash." He instilled that fear into me, and I knew he was right.

When that house payment was due, I sweated it big time. Then the phone would ring. There would be a new referral calling with an order that would more than make up the shortfall I needed to make my payment on time. It happened over and over again—I would need to pay a bill, and the phone would ring with an order.

Each time this miracle happened, I would thank God for the blessing. I was still scared silly and still doubted myself. But as the days rolled into months, my cash flow problems did seem easier.

Those first months were a blur. I just know I worked exceptionally hard; I only left the house to run to the store or make a bank deposit or take Stephen up to see Mom and Pop.

Working seven days a week was the norm, and I knew I was not the mom I used to be. I used to take such an interest in Stephen's homework, teachers, and activities. Now, I barely knew what was going on. It was tough on him, but it was tougher on me because I kept feeling that I was not the parent I once was.

It was a vicious cycle. I was always tired, always worried. Sometimes I had too much empty time, and other times I didn't know how I was going to do it all.

Is There Such a Thing as Enough Working Capital?

I never had enough working capital. I knew this was often the kiss of death especially in a new business. It's not that I hadn't tried to have the spare cash to work with. Taxes, unexpected repairs to equipment, and a hundred other expenses were the norm. Remodeling cost overruns, operating costs and fifty other expenses were not anticipated, but still came along.

I remember my parents talking late into the night as they tried to figure out how to pay the refrigerator repairman when the ice machine acted temperamental. My dad used to get so upset. I was learning exactly how he felt!

Plus, I took such pride in my shop. I went down to the local restaurant/bakery supply house at every opportunity and invested in more and more items that I felt I needed. Everything was purchased on a cash basis.

It simply was not possible to make all the cookies that had been ordered on just the few cookie sheets that I had on hand. I kept telling myself to just have confidence. I needed to believe that when I bought more supplies, the phone would ring with the orders to justify my purchases. I finally took the plunge. Thank the Lord, the phone did ring and ring.

The mixer that Mom gave me was wonderful, but it wasn't enough, so I had to buy another one, then another one, and many more as the years went by. I can proudly say that everything in my shop was really owned by me debt-free.

Even with my constant worrying about money, I owned it all free and clear. I would sit in my shop after closing and survey my surroundings. I would tell myself, "It's all paid for, so quit worrying so much. The phone will ring like crazy tomorrow." And it did.

4

One Customer at a Time,
but Oh Those Lovely Referrals

Let me tell you about Susie, Judy/Sandy, and Cindy.

Susie

I soon developed the reputation for making exceptionally good frosted cutout cookies. After all, that was the basis of my mission statement. There wasn't any place else where buyers could obtain the type and quality of goods that I had. If people could just go down the street to the grocery store and buy the very same items, why would they patronize me?

One afternoon in the late fall, I received a call from a lady named Susie, who told me she lived in the neighborhood of my shop and passed it going to and from work. My sign had intrigued her, and she wanted to check me out. She observed that the sign outside didn't say "Cookies." It just read, "Evie's Bakery Boutique." She then asked, "Do you make really good frosted cutouts?"

I proudly replied, "Yes, I do, and if you would like to stop in, I would be glad to give you one."

She said she wanted to stop in after work and wanted to verify what my shop hours were. I told her and assured her that I looked forward to meeting her.

She came in that afternoon and asked, "Are you Evie?"

"I am indeed. Are you Susie?"

"I'm Susie. I'm here for my free cookie, and it better be good."

I could see that she said it good-naturedly, and I smiled as I handed her a free sample, a frosted flower cutout.

She gratefully bit into it, and I awaited her opinion. She beamed from ear to ear, with frosting in the corner of her mouth. She ate it all and then exclaimed, "You're right, these are the best I have ever had!" She immediately placed her order. Always offer free samples and be willing to listen to what the customer wants. That day, I stood there and enjoyed the satisfaction of realizing that Susie was exactly the kind of customer I was trying to create. Her first question was not price. It was whether they were good, and if so, could she place an order for them. That was the beginning of my friendship with Susie, a nurse in the surgery department at Mercy Hospital. She became one of my Evie ambassadors. She knew many employees at the hospital, and I received referrals because of her. As with most of my customers, we became friends and shared many wonderful moments together.

Judy/Sandy

Word soon hit the street that if you were in sales and needed a break, just cold call Evie. You probably wouldn't make a sale, but you would receive a cookie and a kind word. You would leave her shop feeling better—in your tummy and your psyche.

One day, a tool saleslady named Judy came in. I marveled that a lady could do this job. To this day, I barely know which end of the hammer hits the nail, yet this woman was so well-versed that she could speak expertly and sell a complete line of tools.

I didn't see her that often, but every once in a while, Judy would pop into my shop, and it was always fun to see her. One day, she phoned and asked for an appointment to see me. The anguish in her voice told me that she had trouble. I had no idea what it was, but I knew it was important. I told her that I'd make time for her that afternoon.

Later that day, she came into my shop fighting back the tears. She told me her son had to get married real quick, and she was trying to give him a small wedding. The problem was that she didn't have much money for the arrangements.

She asked if I could possibly make his wedding cake and take a set of tools in lieu of cash payment. It was a lovely set. I looked at the variety of gleaming, exotic tools and had absolutely no idea what I would ever do with them.

But this was a nice lady with a problem. It was within my power to help her, so I told her we had a deal. Without further conversations of gratitude or obligation, I launched into a discussion of cake designs, flavors, number of servings, and delivery time and date.

I gave the tool set to my brother for Christmas, and I think he liked them. He's a handy-andy.

Over the years, I completely forgot the tool set, and as time moved us along different paths, I lost contact with Judy. One day I saw an ad in the paper for a large carpet store that had just opened. There was Judy's picture, but the caption listed her as Sandy. She was still a saleslady, still looking for referrals, and so was I.

I made up a marketing sales bag and cold-called her at the carpet store. As soon as I walked in, she hurried over to me, saying, "Evie, what a surprise to see you!" It was such a compliment that she remembered me. I asked her why the newspaper listed her as Sandy, and she replied that it was her real name. She never used her real name with the tool company job.

She then told me that she had never forgotten the beautiful wedding cake that I made for her son and my kindness in accepting an alternative form of payment.

She has since moved on to real estate sales. Since I'm back in banking, we frequently work together. I provide the financing for her buyers' real estate. And yes, whenever I can, I refer to her as Judy/Sandy!

Cindy

Cindy was another of my first customers. She certainly was an active one! Her family had lots of get-togethers, and the celebration cakes were always ordered from me. Her sister was getting married, and Cindy called me to place the order. She requested if she could stop in to see me and bring a family recipe for me to review. When I looked at the recipe, I really thought there had been a mistake. There was too much buttermilk compared to the amount of flour. I was positive this couldn't be correct. Another instruction that bothered me was the addition of cinnamon and all-spice to a chocolate batter. When I admitted my qualms about these ingredients, Cindy assured me that this recipe was correct. She also said, "You're going to love it." I promised Cindy I would experiment within a few days and let her know the results.

A few days later, I got the opportunity and made a batch. I love chocolate on chocolate, so I frosted off the cake with my chocolate buttercream and also put chocolate buttercream between the layers.

That evening, my son and I went to my mom's for dinner, and we took this cake for our dessert. We devoured it! We had never tasted a cake like this.

I called Cindy the next morning and told her, "Okay, this has got to be the most incredibly unusual and the very best chocolate cake I have ever had. I'll gladly make all of your sister's wedding cake tiers using this recipe *if* you'll let me use this recipe in my shop for other orders."

Cindy graciously replied, "Of course."

It was a blessing to have acquired use of the recipe when I did. Just a few months later, I prepared this batter all day long for my niece Stephanie's wedding cake. There were going to be a lot of guests, and what better type of cake than this fantastic, unusual chocolate dream? After all, Steph was marrying a young man from a family that owned a chocolate factory. I was making Willy Wonka's wedding cake!

I suggested that since it was a June wedding, the cakes should be decorated with lots of buttercream roses and sprigs of pearls. There were also plenty of ruffled buttercream swags. John, an extremely talented local florist, embellished her cake with live roses. The combination of the live roses along with the buttercream gave these cakes an elegance that had never been done before. Later, I was given some small snapshots of the cake, and I used them to start a photo album that I kept on my dining room table in the shop.

* * *

Recipe for Cindy's Cocoa Spice Cake

Single batch will yield two 8-inch rounds or one 12-inch round single batch.

Ingredients

2 teaspoons baking soda
2 cups buttermilk
2 ½ cups white granulated sugar
2 sticks – one cup of either salted sweet cream butter or margarine (I used 1 stick butter and 1 stick margarine)
2 eggs
1 teaspoon vanilla
¼ teaspoon ground cloves
1 teaspoon ground cinnamon
2 tablespoons cocoa (I always use Hershey's)
1 teaspoon ground allspice
3 ¼ cups flour

On a sheet of wax paper, sift the dry ingredients, then set aside.

Pour the buttermilk into a liquid measuring cup. Dissolve the baking soda in this liquid and set aside.

Place the softened butter and margarine into a mixing bowl. Beat at medium speed until blended. Add the sugar, continue to mix, then add the eggs and vanilla. Alternate the dry ingredients with the buttermilk in the creamed mixture and blend.

Pour batter into greased and floured cake pans. Bake at 350 degrees for 30 minutes or until toothpick inserted into the middle comes out clean. Keep in mind, there is a lot of buttermilk in this batter, so your baking time may need to be longer.

Cool pans on a wire rack for 10 minutes. Here is an old trick that a German baker taught me. I know this is going to sound quite strange, but after the cake pans are resting on top of the cooling racks, lay another rack on top and gently press down. Keep those top racks on the entire cooling time. When you go to invert the cake pans, hold them on the sides, keeping the top rack on. Now your cake is inverted onto this rack, lift the pan off, keep the cake on this rack until cool. Then frost with my delicious buttercream frosting.

* * *

Recipe for Buttercream Frosting

(Note: This is my half-batch recipe, the capacity of which should work well in your electric mixer. If you have a five-quart mixer bowl and a Kitchen Aid mixer, go ahead and double it.)

Ingredients

   1/2 cup or 1 stick softened margarine (Parkay or Imperial are my favorites, but use what you prefer.)
   1/2 cup or 1 stick softened salted sweet cream butter
   2 teaspoons vanilla
   2 pounds powdered sugar
   milk (I always used whole milk in the shop, but at home I use skim.)

Directions
   Place margarine, butter, and vanilla in mixer bowl.

Beat thoroughly. Stop mixer, and slowly add about a third of the powdered sugar. Slowly start the mixer, and increase speed without blowing powdered sugar all over the place. Repeat with another third of the sugar. Decrease speed, and slowly add 1 or 2 tablespoons of milk. Mix it well because the secret to fluffy frosting is beating a lot of air into it. Add another tablespoon of milk, and beat like crazy. Reduce mixer speed, and add the remainder of the powdered sugar. Beat like crazy again. You probably need to add a little more milk. This is where judgment and experience come in. The brand of powdered sugar will determine how much milk is needed. A common mistake is to let the frosting mixture get too thick and then try to adjust the consistency by adding more and more milk. It just doesn't work! You need to add a little milk at a time, alternating it with the addition of more powdered sugar until you get the consistency you want.

Store the frosting in an airtight container in the refrigerator for up to three days if you wish.

Note: Chocolate buttercream frosting is made by adding cocoa powder to the frosting you have just made. Remember, as you add cocoa powder, it will absorb the milk you have in the frosting and more milk must be slowly added to keep you consistency correct. How much cocoa powder? I always judge by color. If I wanted a dark frosting, I added a lot of cocoa powder. If I wanted a lighter frosting, I add less.

Reminder: This frosting will darken as it ages.

5

I Take Some Baby Steps—
at Least I'm Walking

Many years before, I found this recipe in my mother's cookbook, *The Joy of Cooking*. This book was given to Mom as a bridal shower gift by her niece, Margaret. Mom treasured this book, and she allowed me to use it. Years later, when Mom's health was slipping, she quietly went about getting her affairs in order. One of the arrangements she was most eager to accomplish was giving me that cookbook. I recently passed it on to my son, Stephen.

When I first tried this recipe, I wondered what would happen if I doubled the amount of baking powder. I found out! That was the secret to moving these cutout cookies beyond the ordinary. Just doubling the baking powder gave the cookies that extra puffiness, and they stayed softer.

Don't be afraid to experiment with a recipe. I can't count the number of times I dumped a batch of something I thought would really be clever, but wasn't. However, the delicious successes I've had with my experiments certainly have justified the effort and expense. (See recipe at the end of the chapter.)

* * *

The two weeks leading up to the first Valentine's Day I was in business were really hectic. Word had begun to get around that Evie made really delicious frosted cutout cookies. There wasn't another bakery anywhere that could beat or even come close to matching my quality.

People were coming into the shop to buy my frosted heart-shaped cutouts. Of course, as all hearts are different, I had my heart-shaped treats frosted in different shades of pink and red.

The process of creating and presenting my cookies simply took time. The cookies had to cool before I could frost them. Then they had to set up before I could arrange them on a plate or in a box.

I had a small shop, and it was filled with waiting cookie customers. There really was only standing room. I offered them complimentary mugs of coffee and tea while they waited. They eagerly accepted. As I raced around, I realized that everyone seemed to be having a great deal of fun. I didn't have time to have fun; I was trying to not go nuts as I dashed around my crowded shop filling orders.

A very thin, nervous lady, a few years my senior, offered to help me serve the beverages. She said her name was Joyce and that she had come in to ask for a job. I told her I just couldn't talk to her with the crush of waiting customers, but if she would wait, I would be happy to talk with her later.

Simple enough. She began passing out beverages. She smiled and seemed to know some of the waiting customers. She kept them pleasantly engaged in conversation while I scurried around my kitchen like a crazy chicken.

Finally, the shop emptied out, and there was Joyce patiently waiting for me. I poured myself a cup of coffee and joined her. I figured I owed her a few minutes after all the help she had been with my crowd control problem. Well, it's a good thing there were no customers left to attend to because Joyce and I talked for two hours.

She explained that for the last twenty-some years, she had been a full-time housewife and mother and then bemoaned, "No one will give me a job!"

I exclaimed, "You mean you're a professional home-maker." She liked that.

Joyce told me of the places she had stopped to seek work. She was looking for only a part-time job. Because of the day I had just had, I realized I needed a part-timer. I had already observed that Joyce was extremely organized and she already knew her way around a kitchen.

I envied her in that I had worked all my life, and she had been living the life I had always wanted. Prior to opening my shop, that is.

She talked about the very large chain store up the road that always had Help Wanted signs in their window but wouldn't hire her because she did not have any retail experience. She said that she frequently shopped there and knew where every piece of merchandise was located. She probably knew the stock better than the young girls who were constantly hired in and out of the place.

I was floored that a large, well-known store could be that foolish. I was so lucky that it was.

Joyce became my confidante and my associate. We had a good fit. Joyce wanted part time, and that's what I could afford. She knew many people in the community and was my best ambassador. Her friends became loyal customers.

My business was developing to the point where my customers often needed their orders delivered. Joyce knew her way around town and was an extremely safe driver. Offering to-the-door delivery became another one of my services to take care of my customers, and no one else did this. I listened to my customer's needs and developed another service for them. That in turn increased my sales.

A member of the police department stopped in to check out my shop and me. When he saw Joyce, he shouted, "Oh thank God, you've taken her off the streets. She's been pedaling her buns around town for years." My Joycie? I was shocked.

He laughed when he saw my expression and explained that Joyce rode her bicycle quite often. It turned out that Joyce's husband, Tom, and our lieutenant were in the same local gun club and had known each other for years.

This was the beginning of a wonderful friendship between the police department and Evie's. We always laughed because the locals always professed that North Canton had no crime!

But I have to tell you, I had always been a little edgy working in my shop all of those crazy hours in the very early morning. I never felt scared of being in my shop after the police unofficially adopted Evie's. Many nights, the officers would drive through my parking lot and flash their bright lights. I'd go to the window and wave. They would do this a few times a night.

They made sure I was safe and secure. I made sure that three boxes filled to the brim with goodies from my shop would find their way to the police station periodically. The boxes were marked "Morning Shift," "Afternoon Shift," and "Third Shift."

I have always been a hands-on manager. It was easier to have Joyce make the deliveries and the grocery store runs.

She knew the layout of the grocery store better than me and dashed through it with my list and was back pronto. I gave her a business check for the payment. She was never questioned when she wrote the checks. That was okay with me.

One Sunday afternoon, I went to the grocery store for supplies and wrote a check for the purchase. The clerk looked at me and said, "So, what's she like?"

I had no clue what she was talking about and asked her what she meant by that question.

She replied, "You know, what's she really like?"

Again, I asked for an explanation to her question.

The clerk persisted, "You know, the real Evie." What's she really like?"

I laughed and smiled and said, "I'm Evie. Why do you ask?"

"Oh no, I mean the real Evie. What's she really like? She comes in here and runs through the aisles, zips through checkout and races out the door. Does she do everything so fast all the time?"

I was cracking up! It was good to know that my employee was not a time waster and a master at time management. I took out my driver's license and showed it to the clerk. Emphatically and trying not to laugh, I exclaimed, "I'm the real Evie."

She was in shock and said, "But then, who's that woman?"

I told her that she was my employee, Joyce. I could hardly wait to tell Joyce about the clerk discovering the real Evie.

Joyce and I just howled over that incident with each cup of coffee we drank for months on end, and I reminded her that I was the real Evie.

* * *

Evie's Cutout Cookies

This is for a double batch. I never made just a single batch. Yield is dependent upon size of cutters; regular-sized hearts make about 10 dozen.

Ingredients

- 2 sticks of softened salted sweet cream butter and 2 sticks of Imperial or Parkay margarine - 2 cups
- 1 ½ cups of white granulated sugar
- 2 teaspoons of vanilla
- 2 eggs
- 4 teaspoons of baking powder (the original recipe called for half of this)
- 6 cups of flour (I always use Gold Medal for my cookies and piecrust)

Cream the butter/margarine and sugar. Don't overwork this mixture. Add the eggs one at a time, mix, add the baking powder. Mix then add the flour. If you have the type of mixer I have, you can add 3 cups, whirl mixer until flour is integrated with the sugar butter batter. Then add the other 3 cups of flour. If you have a smaller capacity mixer, then cut this recipe in half. Scrape the mixer paddle and bowl, remove batter, and put into a mixing bowl. Cover with plastic wrap and refrigerate until stiff enough to work with.

Many people cannot successfully roll out cutout cookies, but I use my mother's secret. Too much flour on your counter will produce tough cookies, so lightly sprinkle flour on your rolling surface—kitchen counter. Then place a mound of dough, pat down and cover the dough with a sheet of plastic wrap, roll out to desired thickness. Make sure you dip your cookie cutters into flour—I keep mine on the side of my rolling-out area. Place the cutouts about 2 inches apart on an ungreased baking sheet, bake at 350 degrees for 6 minutes, then rotate the cookie sheets; in other words, if you have 2 sheets in an oven at a time, which is what I do, take the top sheet and place it on the rack below after removing the bottom sheet. Place the bottom sheet on the top rack. Bake for another 4–6 minutes. Gas ovens give a light brown color, and electric ovens don't. My father always preferred a gas oven, and so do I.

If you are unsure if the cookies are baked enough, remove the tray and place on a wire rack (adjacent if possible) on a counter next to your stove, gently lift up one cookie, and if it is lightly browned, the cookie is baked. After baking, remove the cookie sheets and place on wire racks to cool. Scrape the cookies gently as soon as you take them out of the oven. When cool, frost with my buttercream frosting, wait until they are set up/dry, then place in food safe storage containers. I usually line mine with plastic wrap and put sheets of wax paper between the layers. These cookies freeze wonderfully and will stay in your freezer for up to 3 months.

6

Customers Do Not Live by Cookies Alone

Not everyone was raised the way I was. I grew up with parents that cooked and prepared everything from scratch.

When my mother was going to have guests over to our house, it would never have occurred to her in a thousand years to call someone for help. She also would never have dreamed of going to visit one of her friends empty-handed.

Mother always baked scrumptious pies and cookies to take to our friends. Likewise, when mother's friends came to visit us, they always brought abundant goodies too. We knew what to expect when Irene or Polly came over. Irene was my beautiful godmother who was a very talented Greek cook and baker. She made delightfully delicious dishes and pastries that Mom didn't make. All of us knew that we were in for lots of Greek hospitality filled with scrumptious food and desserts. Polly was an Italian married to Andy, who is Mom and Pop's Greek friend. We had never had homemade Italian spaghetti noodles before; Polly always made her Italian dishes from scratch. Her cooking was different from ours, and we waited with great anticipation knowing we were in for lots of surprising different foods. Interestingly enough, all of these ladies did different goodies. And these were good goodies!

But fortunately, there are lots of people who either do not have the talent or the time to prepare everything when they have guests over. These were the customers I sought and found. Then I listened to them when they ordered their desserts from me.

But they wanted more than desserts. So I always referred them to my favorite caterer in town, but invariably, they would say, "Evie, do you just have a spread I could serve with some crackers and a drink? I just want something easy. We're meeting at our house, and then we're going out to dinner."

Well sure, I did. But then I needed to call my sales rep from the local wholesaler to provide paper goods and packaging. I called Tom, and sure enough, he had several items he thought would do the job quite nicely. He suggested a new product. It was clear plastic clamshells with attached dome lids. I ordered a case and then wondered what I was going to do with 250 of them!

"Have faith" is easy to say, but when you have to write the checks to pay for inventory, your faith is in for a severe test. I started letting my customers know that I had two fantastic cracker spreads, just in case they needed something special. I also told my busy customers they would make an excellent solution to giving that hostess gift they had been searching for. I tied beautiful bows on them using seasonal ribbons. Faith, and spreading the word about my cracker spreads, did the job. The response was phenomenal. Soon, those orders came in.

I needed extra shelf space in my refrigerator to place the orders waiting for pick up. Buying another refrigerator was not in the year's budget, so I was forced to limit the number of orders I filled, especially at my peak Thanksgiving and Christmas season.

It was the second week in December, and I had just announced to my employees that no one was to take any more orders. I had just reconciled the order box and realized that there were lots of hours already booked, and we could not do any more.

I took a phone call from a lady who was really upset when I told her I could not take any more holiday orders, which included my apple cheddar cheese cracker spread. Her reply was, "Now what am I supposed to do? I already promised my neighbor I would bring the crackers and spread to her house this Saturday night for our annual neighborhood get-together. She was so excited when I told her I was bringing Evie's spread. Fine, just give me the recipe, and I'll make it myself!" I told her that I did not give out my recipes, and she was absolutely furious. Not only did she chew me out, but she also slammed the phone. I felt terrible, but there simply was no way to do anything for her.

I hope this woman is reading this because here is my infamous apple cheddar cheese recipe. I saw this recipe in a newspaper many years ago. It has always been a favorite in my family. As a bonus, I am including my mother-in-law Flavia's blue cheese ball recipe. It was given to her by a co-worker. It is my brother Bill's favorite.

* * *

Apple Cheddar Spread

1–8 ounces softened cream cheese
½ cup mayonnaise
½ cup shredded sharp cheddar cheese
½ cup finely chopped unpeeled apple

Place cream cheese and mayonnaise into mixer bowl. Whirl at medium speed until blended. Then add cheese and apples. Gently blend. This mixture can be scraped into your favorite serving dish/bowl. Keep refrigerated until serving time. This spread is delicious over crackers, pear or apple slices. It is particularly pretty if the bowl is placed on a wood-carved board surrounded by crackers and whole apples and pears with small paring knives. Small serving dishes adjacent to the carving board and decorator napkins make a lovely appetizer centerpiece on your table.

Can be made a day ahead of serving.

* * *

Flavia's Blue Cheese Ball

A single batch will make 3 smaller balls or one large one.

½ of a 12-ounce can of pitted large black olives—chopped and drained and blotted in paper towels
1 8-ounce package of cream cheese and ½ of an 8-ounce package of cream cheese or 12 ounces of cream cheese
1 stick of margarine – ½ cup
4 tablespoons mayonnaise

½ teaspoon of garlic salt
½ teaspoon of Worcestershire sauce
4 ounce package of crumbled blue cheese

Place cream cheese, margarine, and mayonnaise in mixing bowl. Whirl at medium speed with electric mixer. Add the garlic salt and Worcestershire sauce. Whirl until mixed, remove paddle, scrap down sides of bowl with rubber spatula. By hand, add in the olives and blue cheese.

Scrape contents onto waxed sheet in a pan, refrigerate until hardened. Then shape into balls and roll in finely chopped walnuts or pecans or finely chopped parsley (due to the fact that some people are allergic to nuts and also considering their cost, I always roll my balls in parsley).

Store finished balls in container in the refrigerator. Must make ahead of time. 1–2 days before serving is ideal. I love items that can be made ahead of serving time.

7

Giving Away Your Smarts
Opens Their Hearts

When I first opened my shop, I needed to get people in. I had heard that a very talented gourmet chef in a little town north of me was giving very expensive lessons in the evening. Well, if she could teach gourmet cooking, maybe I could show some people how to make old-fashioned apple dumplings.

Mom flipped out. She couldn't understand why I would show people how to do what I could do. She wondered why they would still order from me once they knew how to do it themselves. I tried to reassure her that my clientele was just looking for something fun to do. They would not do it themselves in a million years.

I called one of my very good apple dumpling customers and asked her if she had some friends along with their spouses that would like to learn how to make apple dumplings. Men love apple dumplings! She cracked up and the next day called to tell me she had lined up six couples. I scrubbed my already clean kitchen and got everything prepped. I was ready to go.

The husbands had more fun than anybody. I had them making piecrust mix and rolling out squares of dough. Then I showed them how I cut free hand with a small paring knife the leaves that I attached to the tops of the dumplings. They paid their fees and took their freshly baked apple dumplings home. After they left, I dragged myself upstairs and collapsed into bed.

The next morning, Linda, the organizer of the student group, called to tell me that she had already heard that the class was an enormous hit. Every one was raving about the good time they had, and she assured me that they would become future customers.

Then Linda asked me if she could order twenty apple dumplings.

"Linda, were you or were you not in my class last night"?

She laughed and replied, "Evie, you don't think I'd do all that work, do you?" My plan worked, and I could hardly wait to call Mother!

*   *   *

Piecrust Recipe

Yield 2 pie shells and 1 top...and a little extra.

Ingredients

　　4 cups flour (I prefer Gold Medal.)
　　2 teaspoons salt
　　1 2/3 cups Crisco Butter Flavor shortening

Directions
Measure these ingredients into a large bowl, and using a pastry blender, chop or cut into the size of small peas. You

can use two table knives and use a cutting motion until the desired consistency. If you don't have a pastry blender, invest in one. It's much easier to use than two table knives.

You are doing this by hand. The secret to flaky piecrust is adding your initial ice water all at once and not overworking your dough when you mix it. Add four tablespoons of ice water right at the beginning of the mixing. As soon as it looks like you can roll it out, stop. Do not overwork. If it needs more water, add some more. But as soon as it can be formed into a ball, you are ready to roll out your piecrust.

This is the way my mom did it when I was a little girl. Mother would sprinkle some flour onto the kitchen counter. She would place a ball of dough on this surface. She would pat it down and then lay a sheet of waxed paper on the top. Then she would roll out to about 1/8 of an inch. Carefully she would run a wide pancake turner utensil under the dough until all the dough had been loosened from the surface. Using her utensil and her hand, she gently laid the dough into her pie shell. Then she slowly removed the waxed paper and eased the dough into the pie pan. She trimmed around the pie pan, leaving about a one-inch excess, which she tucked under the pie pan rim.

I always liked Mother's fluting. It was a standup fluting rather than a flat one. She put her right index finger inside the rim and her left index finger and thumb on the outside. Her left finger and thumb pinched the pastry into a V shape, but she didn't allow her left fingers to come together. She saved a space to insert her right index finger to push the dough into the V space as the left fingers gently pinched her right finger. This is the way I do it too, except I replaced the waxed paper with plastic food wrap.

Mother never made her pie mix ahead. When Mom was going to make a pie, it often turned out to be eight or ten pies, all made in one long session. She was always generous with friends and relatives, and they loved her pies. We kids were lucky if one of the pies remained on our kitchen table for us.

I always made my piecrust mix in advance. I had to plan ahead. This recipe is a perfect plan-ahead tool. The mixture can be stored in an airtight container at room temperature for up to six months. Be sure to label it "piecrust mix" and add the date it was made. (add cold water when ready to use). When I had a big holiday or a big pie day coming up on my calendar, I would make many, many batches of this piecrust mix beforehand.

Now back to giving out my recipes to students. Several weeks after my apple dumpling class, I called Mother and invited her to accompany me to a very large brand-new home in a very prominent neighborhood. I was going to demonstrate how to make my Peanut Butter Pops to a ladies group.

I had instructed the hostess in regard to the necessary ingredients. She assured me that she would have everything that I had listed. She told me that about twenty of her friends would be there. I wondered how large of a kitchen she had to accommodate such a crowd.

Mother told me I was really goofy to give away my recipe and technique for making these really different cookies. Especially since no one, and I mean no one, was making this fantastic cookie.

I assured Mother that these ladies needed something different to occupy their monthly meeting. I told her I'd bet her a penny that they probably would never make them, especially when they knew how simple ordering them from Evie's shop could be.

I saw it as free advertising for me. Mother agreed to go with me, and we all had the best time. The ladies could not have been more gracious. The kitchen was so huge I just couldn't believe my eyes. I shared a knowing wink with my mother as we learned that none of them really spent any time in the similar huge kitchens in their homes.

At the beginning of the evening, I only knew the hostess. She made sure everyone got to know me, and she also made it her private mission to see that each and every one of her friends became an Evie's customer.

Moral of this story: I have never been afraid to share a recipe since that evening.

* * *

Peanut Butter Cookie Pop Dough Recipe

This is for a single batch. Just remember, 1/2 and 1/2, and you'll have this recipe memorized.

 1 stick of softened salted sweet cream butter (½ cup)
 ½ cup of white granulated sugar
 ½ cup of brown sugar
 ½ teaspoon of vanilla
 ½ cup of Jif peanut butter (the only kind I use)
 1 egg
 ½ teaspoon of baking power
 ½ teaspoon of baking soda
 1 ½ cups of flour

Place into an electric mixer bowl the butter, white sugar, brown sugar, vanilla, and peanut butter. Mix on medium speed until almost blended, add the baking power and soda, and whirl. Add the egg, whirl. Then add the flour and mix until combined, scrape paddle and bowl and place batter into bowl. Cover and refrigerate until batter is workable to scoop out onto cookie sheets. Bake at 350 degrees on an ungreased cookie sheet, allowing space for the cookies to spread slightly while baking. Yes, you can crisscross them with a floured fork for a traditional peanut butter cookie or insert a snack-size Snickers bar inside the scoop of batter, roll slightly to cover the candy bar, then place on the cookie sheet.

Here's where it gets more unique. Insert a white cookie stick into the candy piece, wrap the scoop of dough around the cookie. Carefully place cookies apart from each other on the cookie sheet. Bake for 6 minutes, then rotate the 2 cookie sheets from top of bottom shelf and bake for an additional 4–6 minutes. These cookies are "foolers." The bottoms can burn because you don't think the tops are brown enough, so be careful. Create something really special by using a small scoop and crisscross cookies, then make sandwiches with baked cookies having buttercream frosting between them. Then dip ½ of the sandwich in melted chocolate. The peanut butter snickers can be ½ dipped in melted chocolate too. My customers went crazy over these. Each Christmas, I had a very well-know surgeon who ordered a huge 7-dozen platter of these peanut butter Snickers for his annual party at his office. This is the best-tasting peanut butter cookie dough I have found.

8

Lots of Red Didn't Bring
Lots of Green

In my third year, as the big holidays approached, I was eager to find some way to increase sales. I had been mulling over an idea I hoped might do the trick. More and more of my customers had been requesting a cookie list, and I came to believe that such a list might be very helpful, if not crucial, to achieving increased cookie sales.

I can't remember where I had learned it, but I knew that prior customers combined with current customers would prove to be my most dependable customer base. Any future success I hoped to reach would have to start with that rock-solid base. It just made sense to me. These people knew who I was, where I was, and what I was providing. I had already done my best to give them an outstanding baked-goods experience.

Everyone has heard that word of mouth is the best advertisement. That made sense to me. No matter how elaborate a TV commercial or a newspaper advertisement may be, you know that behind it, someone has *paid* those people (usually actors) to say wonderful things about the product in question. On the other hand, suppose someone spends their own money to buy one of my cookies and then goes to a friend and says, "Boy did I have a terrific cookie yesterday. It was from Evie's." Then you've got something powerful. Not only is the person's money involved but also their reputation in a friend's eyes.

All of this meant that I had to put out a cookie list! I would mail a comprehensive list of my cookie offerings to my existing customer base. My hope was that they would come to my shop for another visit, and that they would tell their friends about me. It seemed like a good plan to me. All I needed was the list. It needed to be an enticing one.

My friend Bernie, from the local newspaper, always said, "When you come up with that price list, let me know, and I'll print if for you." I had never done anything like this, but I could visualize what I wanted. The problem would be getting it on paper for Bernie to print.

These were the days before I owned my own personal computer. So it was that I set out on my first major advertising venture. In every spare moment that I could find, I would retrieve my notes and then write something. Not only did my flyer have pricing; it accurately described the cookies, especially the ones that were a part of my family's recipes.

I wrote a copy, selected an artwork, and designed, laid out, and changed my flyer around using the old cut-and-paste method. Everything was done by hand. I must confess that I have very poor handwriting. When I was at the bank, the staff wouldn't accept handwritten memos from me. I had to type all of my messages and input slips.

My hodgepodge flyer was finally done. I called Bernie and set an appointment to show it to him. The North

Canton Sun was just down the street, so I was able to slip away for a short time.

Poor Bernie. He looked at the piece I had labored over for more than a week, and his brow furrowed. Oh my gosh. What had I done wrong? Bernie spoke hesitantly. "Evie, I'm sorry. I just can't read this." I was relieved that we had a solvable problem. I had to read every inch of my creation to him.

It turns out I had not done a bad job of cobbling my flyer together. Once I interpreted my handwriting, we moved along quite nicely. I hadn't given any thought to choice of paper color. Bernie showed me my options, and I felt like a kid in a candy store. Then the obvious choice hit my eye. "Let's flood the post office with red," I told my printer. A few days later, Bernie brought me my proof copy, and I was thrilled. My flyer had turned out even better than I had imagined.

Working in the bank had taught me the value of keeping careful and complete records. It helped me a great deal when I opened my bakeshop. I had taken the time to keep records of my customers' purchases on index cards. Most of my sales were preordered, and most of my customers paid by check. These cards were my CPC cards—customer profile cards. Not only did this practice create a mailing list but also gave me the basis for future sales, without depending on my memory. The time-consuming effort of maintaining ongoing records of customer transactions on my CPC's was worth it. I am proud to say that by the time I closed my shop, I had a very large filing cabinet filled with these cards. However, today's computer/cash registers have point-of-purchase sales capture. The clerk gets your zip code, phone number, and so on, and never saying, "Thank you for stopping in today." It's efficient, but I find it too impersonal for building a business the way I did.

The sales from the fall season paid for the flyers and the postage. I had the policy of paying for everything I did on a cash basis. I was determined to not overextend myself in an effort to grow.

Bernie promptly delivered five hundred beautiful red flyers to me, and I started folding and addressing them each day between all my other activities. Each night, I made myself sit down and work on them for one hour before I dragged myself up the steps and collapsed into bed. I also spent all day Sunday working on them. Even if someone had volunteered to help with this chore, I couldn't have used help. I knew no one could decipher my CPC's, so I just did it all.

I guess the post office got them delivered. That fact was verified by my friend David, the mailman, who stopped into my shop and said, "Hey, Evie, what are you doing? Everything in my bag is red. In fact the entire post office is red! What's up?" Laughingly, I said, "Didn't you read them?"

David was shocked. "Are you kidding? I'm not allowed to read the mail!"

I had some extras on my counter, so I gave one to David to read. He was very impressed.

I had mailed the flyers out two weeks before Thanksgiving, hoping to capture Thanksgiving sales as well. That's why I listed pies on this cookie list. The phone started ringing off the hook immediately. Most people, whether they like pumpkin pie or not, feel they have to have a pumpkin pie for Thanksgiving. Those orders came in as expected, but what took me by surprise was the enthusiastic clamor for my new offering, Kentucky Bourbon apple pie.

I knew no one else in town offered this pie. It was a winner. I peeled and sliced apples until I thought I'd lose my mind. I had the black hands to prove it.

It was the response I had been eager for. I had prayed for this response and thought I was prepared. I was not! You see, I had plastic buckets of piecrust mix already prepared and ready to go. I had my two freezers filled with already baked cookies for my "just in case." I figured if I didn't sell everything, I'd worry about what to do with the leftovers later. *Leftovers?*

I had so many Thanksgiving orders, for mostly pies and cookies, the first week after my flyer hit my customers' homes that I had to stop taking Thanksgiving orders. By the middle of December, I simply could not take any more Christmas orders.

I found out that customers do not want to be told no. They were irate on the phone when they heard me say I just could not take any more orders. Believe me, it broke my heart to turn then down.

Some other things I'd always heard actually are true:

1. There really are only twenty-four hours in a day.

2. As the Chinese say, "Be careful what you wish for. You might get it!"

New Year's Day, I sat down and reconciled my orders with the money that I had invested on the flyers and postage. It was not a profitable picture. The mailers obviously did their job, bringing in eager customers. I just did not have the man hours available to respond to this new, overwhelming demand.

The one good thing about learning the hard way is that you *do* learn lessons that you are not likely to forget. Spending money to make money is good, but spending money and *not* making money is bad.

I decided to rethink advertising expenditures and concentrate on more controllable customer growth. I must tell you though, that years later, I still had people refer to "those red Christmas flyers" when they called to order. Perhaps, the expense of this project has been amortized over many years.

I also learned that there was a huge desire for what I had to offer in my bakeshop. I simply needed to get better prepared to handle the large number of people who were looking for bakery products of the quality I demanded of myself.

I realized that I never had to advertise again because of word-of-mouth referrals. They really do work. Slow but steady growth became my business objective. I stayed within the boundaries of what I was able to handle, and my business flourished. I did very well.

In the process, I learned about the unseen world of connections. My patrons just always wanted to tell me things. Small world indeed! I learned which customers were friends, which were related, which were enemies. It was fun (and profitable) to know who was who and what was what. Like a good bartender, I never ever breached a confidentiality.

* * *

Recipe for Kentucky Bourbon Apple Pie

I received this recipe in a free book that I sent for, which was advertised on a package of almonds. I have found that some of my best recipes were on the backs of labels on the products that I was using.

This is a really different way to prepare an apple pie filling. Do not doubt that this is the correct method. It sure helps to have a husband with a strong arm who can whip in the cornstarch like my dear Ron does for me at home. Where was he in the early days when I could have used his help?

This is for a single batch, which is a very generous 9-inch pie. Have an unbaked pie shell ready.

7 cups of peeled sliced apples
1 tablespoon of lemon juice (I use bottled)
1 cup white granulated sugar
½ teaspoon of allspice
½ teaspoon of cinnamon
¼ cup of bourbon (this really is the pièce de résistance)
4–6 tablespoons of cornstarch
Streusel Topping (make before you prepare the filling and then set aside)
1 cup flour
½ cup brown sugar
1 stick of salted sweet cream butter

Using a pastry blender or 2 butter knives, place flour, sugar, and softened butter into bowl and cut into small crumbly mixture. Then add 1/8 cup of almonds. Arrange this mixture on top of the filled pie. Bake at 425 degrees for 15 minutes, then reduce heat to 350 degrees and bake for an additional 40 minutes until the juices from the filling start to bubble up through the top.

Helpful hint:

Make the apple mixture early in the day. Every hour or so, stir it so that the apples marinate in the bourbon. Into a large mixing bowl, place the apples, lemon juice, sugar, allspice, cinnamon, and bourbon. Stir with a large spoon. After this mixture marinates for a minimum 2 hours, then drain reserve liquid in cooking pot, place the drained apples back into the marinating bowl. Bring the reserved liquid to a boil; and slowly, using a wire whip, 1 tablespoon at a time, whisk in about 4–6 tablespoons of cornstarch, do not overcook. The mixture should be a gravy consistency. Remove the boiling mixture off of the heat and fold in the drained apples. Pour this mixture into your crust-prepared pie pan. Top with crumbled topping.

9

It's a Wicker, Wicker World

Growing up in a Greek household, I have strong memories of what the holidays meant to me. Except for some of the details, I suspect they represent wonderful magical times to all little kids.

Memorial Day (called Decoration Day in those days), Fourth of July, Labor Day, Halloween, and Thanksgiving meant fun and family and good times.

But the two holidays that you circled on the big calendar in your mind were Christmas and Easter. Weeks and weeks of planning and preparation went into those two days. As they neared, there was electricity in the very air that made you tingle. You would go to sleep thinking about the approaching holiday and then you'd dream about it. Of course, for weeks before, any kid worth his salt could tell you exactly how many days remained until the big day.

The reasons why I remember these holidays with such fondness are my mom's baking and my Pop's cooking. And of course, my heart swells every time I remember the love that lit every corner of our house.

I remember Easter meant Pop was making a fabulous lamb dinner, and you got a special basket. It was packed with colored cellophane grass and filled with so much chocolate that even a certified chocoholic like me would be satisfied. I loved the basket as much as all the treasures it held. It was a magical basket that was retrieved by mother from our attic every Easter eve and placed on the kitchen table before we went to bed. Easter morning, we would run downstairs and find our baskets overflowing with chocolate treats of every description. The Easter bunny had done it again!

I loved baskets. I decided at the beginning of my shop that baskets would be a major type of presentation on special occasion orders. But I knew that my baskets needed to stand apart from the candy-filled baskets everyone knew so well. I dared to try something different.

A basket from Evie's was filled with made-from-scratch muffins, small breads, and cookies, all individually wrapped and bowed. I just knew this was a really good idea. Why? Because it was unique! No one else was doing it. This was the essence of my shop.

I knew for sure I would include Mom's banana bread, Joyce's carrot-pineapple bread, and Mary Regula's bran muffins. (All of these recipes can be found at the end of this chapter.)

Joyce was kind enough to share the carrot-pineapple bread recipe with me. It was given to her by one of her friends. I needed to test it on someone other than myself. When my son, Stephen, came home from school, I told him I had a taste test for him to perform. I handed him a slice of the bread slathered with some butter and a glass of milk and watched his reaction as he took a big bite of the bread. His face immediately lit up. "Mom," he said, "what is this?" I knew I had a winner for my baskets.

Joycie also gave me Mary's recipe book and said, "Just try these bran muffins." I told her that I had already tried all the bran muffin recipes, and they were all dreadful. Bran may be good for you, but it tastes awful!

I took Joycie's advice and made a batch, and Joyce was so right. I was so excited. I immediately contacted Mary and asked if she would mind me using her recipe. Mary was the wife of our district's former long-time congressman. She gave me her permission in person. She came into my shop, and I was so pleased to meet such a gracious lady.

* * *

George was an advertising sales rep who had made a cold call on me right before Valentine's Day. I turned down the offer to advertise in his magazine for two strong reasons: I had no idea what business would be like for Valentines Day, and I didn't have the money.

I had a fear in the back of my head that George was a good salesman. That meant he would be persistent. I was right. After Valentine's Day, he showed up at my shop to discuss placing an ad in his magazine for Easter.

I didn't really resent his coming by again. As a matter of fact, I admired his skills. He was determined and not easily defeated. He was a good listener, and he struck me as sincere. My problem was the constant lack of money to invest in advertising of any sort.

I gave George a cup of coffee and a free cookie, and we chatted while I worked around the kitchen. He genuinely seemed to like my shop and wanted me to succeed. I knew I was telling him what so many others had already told him: no money to advertise.

He solicited my ideas, and he listened. Since talking about my ideas didn't cost anything, I gave him plenty. I also showed him the cute little baskets my brother had given me. I thought a lot of people might like a small affordable basket of goodies for Easter. George told me that a lot of people were in the market for a ten-dollar gift basket.

The problem I saw was that if I invested in baskets and they didn't sell, what was I going to do with a couple of cartons of little baskets? I didn't have the extra cash to put into inventory, let alone place an ad in his magazine.

George smiled and said, "I think you have an inflated idea of how much a small ad in my magazine will cost you." Then he drew a small ad that I could run in his magazine for ten dollars!

I was hooked. The little ad that George had drawn up simply stated my business name, address, and phone number. It also said, "Made from scratch muffins, cookies, and breads, all individually wrapped. Baskets priced from $10 and higher. Call to order yours today."

Then there occurred one of those moments you remember for the rest of your life! In one fantastic suggestion, he solved both the problem of not having the extra cash to purchase baskets as well as erasing my fear of somehow scraping together money to invest in baskets and then being stuck with them if they didn't sell.

"You know, Evie, my wife has a basement full of baskets that she's received over the years, and she has no idea what to do with any of them. Why don't you tell people that they can drop off *their* baskets, and you'll fill them with *your* delicious goodies? This should solve your dilemma of investing in any inventory."

I truly thought I was going to keel over! I could barely catch my breath and say, "Oh my gosh." George quickly scribbled an additional line to my ad. "Bring your gift baskets in, and Evie will fill them for you with her delicious homemade goodies." Now, I had a golden opportunity to sell more products...with practically no investment of funds!

Although the ad only ran once, I thought I would lose my mind. People started coming in and dropping off baskets. Carefully, I tagged each basket with the owner's name and suggested how I could create a special gift for them.

In the midst of this basket landslide, two baskets came in that really were (to be kind) kind of ugly. Joycie cracked up when she saw them and dared me to turn them into beautiful gifts, worthy of the Evie's label.

These two monstrosities were the toughest challenge in this whole project, but when I was finished, I am proud to say that both Joycie and I really liked the look of them. When my customer came to pick them up, she was bowled over. Secretly, I have always believed she thought this was a way to get rid of these unattractive baskets someone had given her. She must have hated them too. It was a thrill for me to turn these two piles of weird wickers into desirable gifts.

My brother had given me twenty of those little ten-dollar baskets to get rid of. A lady, whose husband was a well-known physician in town, called and ordered all twenty—sight unseen for his large office staff.

She had never even been in my shop but had heard about me. These ten-dollar gifts were the perfect solution to her continuing problem of finding something in this price range for her husband's staff.

She became a wonderful customer after that. Not only did she order for her husband's staff, she gifted her family and friends through my shop. I also received many personal referrals from her, which resulted in many additional orders.

What about those little brown ten-dollar baskets? The phone rang off the hook from that one small ad in George's magazine. Call after call, I had to repeat that they were sold out. I was quite concerned that I would be accused of some kind of bait-and-switch scam. However, that didn't happen. As a matter of fact, every one of the callers apologized to me for not calling sooner!

George stopped in soon after the magazine had been distributed, but I was too busy writing up orders to talk to him or thank him properly for his brilliant ideas. Soon after, I heard that George had quit his job, sold his home, and moved to Florida. I regret I was never able to tell George that he was the smartest ad man I'd ever met. He really was.

The success of my Easter basket experiment reinforced the concept of my three prime rules.

Three Prime Rules

1. Build a product or service that no one else has!

2. Strive to be creative.

3. Don't fear failure.

* * *

Mom's Banana Bread

I never knew where Mom got this recipe, but this is the banana bread that she always made for us. Mom wrote this recipe down on a piece of paper. I inserted it into my procedure book and never did retype it in proper format.

Ingredients

2 cups flour

1 teaspoon soda

1/2 cup or 1 stick softened salted sweet cream butter

1 cup white sugar

2 eggs

1 cup mashed bananas, which is usually about 2 medium-sized ones

1/3 cup milk

1 teaspoon of vinegar or lemon juice (I always use white vinegar) place the vinegar into the milk and set aside.

1 teaspoon of banana extract

Directions

Into your electric mixer bowl, place the butter and sugar and beat until smooth. Reduce mixer speed. Add the eggs and whirl. Add the bananas, banana extract, and soda and beat until smooth. Put the mixer on a slow speed and alternately add the flour and milk mixture until blended.

You can add 1/2 cup chopped nuts if desired. I never did because so many people cannot tolerate nuts in their diet.

Spray the bread pans with cooking spray, and bake in the oven at 350 degrees until a wooden toothpick inserted into the middle comes out clean.

For small loaves, about 15–20 minutes. For a regular-sized bread loaf, the time may go to almost an hour. If your bread is turning golden and it's not done yet, lay a sheet of foil on top to prevent excessive browning.

Remove the loaves from the oven and place on a rack to cool. Run a sharp knife around the edges of the pans. Allow cooling for 10 minutes, and place another rack on top of the pans. Then holding the bottom rack and top rack together, invert, remove the pans, place another rack on top, hold both racks, and invert again. Cool and wrap.

The small loaves fit in small plastic sandwich bags and can be bowed at the ends. For the large size, wrap in plastic food wrap.

These already wrapped breads can be placed in freezer bags and will keep in the freezer for up to three months.

Evie's tip: When bananas are on sale, just put them in the freezer as is. When it is time to make the breads, put them on a plate and microwave to defrost. Peel and place on another plate and smash with a fork.

* * *

Joyce's Carrot-Pineapple Bread

Single batch. Yield: 15 small bread loaves, 1 large or 2 medium-sized pans

  3 eggs
  2 cups of white sugar
  1 cup of grated carrots (Hint: When carrots are on sale, buy them! Peel and grate then place into freezer bags and flatten the bags so that they are not mounded. This makes access to them much easier when you need to use them. Then all you have to do is scoop, measure and thaw to use in your recipes. I always did this and you will appreciate having these carrots ready to go in the freezer)
  1 cup of crushed, drained pineapple
  2 teaspoons of vanilla
  1 ½ teaspoons of cinnamon
  1 teaspoon of baking soda

3 cups flour
1 cup chopped nuts (This is optional. I never used them
   due to my fear of a patron being allergic to nuts.)

Into a large mixing bowl, add the eggs and whip with a
large mixing fork, add the sugar, then the oil, stirring vigor-
ously until blended. Then add the pineapple, vanilla, cinnamon, and soda. Stir until blended. Add the flour and stir
until mixed thoroughly. Then add the optional nuts. Pour
into greased bread pans. I always use PAM cooking spray
because I love the convenience. Due to the large amount of
oil, these breads take longer to bake than you would think.
Be careful to not fill your pans too high because this bread
does rise. Bake at 350 degrees. After removing the pans
from the oven, cook on wire racks. Run a sharp knife around
the tops and down the sides of the pans. Cool for 10 minutes. Invert the pans onto another cooling rack. Complete
the cooling process. Individually wrap in plastic wrap; they
can be placed in freezer bags or give them as gifts.

If you have a son like my Stephen, watch out, they will
disappear before you can do anything with them.

* * *

Mary's Buttermilk Bran Muffins

Guaranteed to be the very best you will ever taste. The neat
thing is you can store a covered bucket of this batter in your
refrigerator for up to 4 days and bake off as needed. I never
tried freezing these muffins, so I have not suggested that
you do this. The following is for ½ batch; you can easily
double this recipe if desired. I always made a single batch.

2 cups Kellogg's All-Bran
1 cup of Nabisco 100% Bran
1 cup boiling water
2 cups buttermilk
1 ½ cups granulated white sugar
½ cup shortening (I always use Crisco)
2 eggs
2 ½ teaspoons baking soda
2 ½ cups flour

Measure 2 cups of Kellogg's All-Bran cereal and 1 cup of Nabisco 100% Bran into a very large mixing bowl. By hand, add a cup of boiling water. Stir until thoroughly mixed with a large spoon. Add buttermilk and stir until blended. Set mixture aside.

Into your electric mixer bowl, place sugar and shortening. Beat until smooth, add eggs, and mix thoroughly. Scrape down sides of bowl with rubber spatula. Add eggs. Place this mixture into the cereal mixture by hand, add the baking soda and flour.

Either spray the muffin tins or use paper liners. Bake at 375 degrees for 14 minutes depending on oven types. Use a wooden toothpick inserted into the center to test for doneness. The pick should be clean when removed. Due to the large amount of buttermilk, do not be surprised that the muffins take longer than other kinds.

Remove pans from oven and cool on wire rack. Or eat while still warm. You won't be able to wait to pop them into your mouth.

10

I've Sown the Seed,
Where's the Crop?

It was obvious I needed referrals to be successful. I believed that since I was making quality goods in a lovely unique setting, it would be a natural for anyone who used my bakery to recommend it to their friends. And the plan was working. I was getting new customers from existing customers. I wanted the process to expand.

I needed to get business accounts and referrals from businesses. I decided to approach related businesses. Caterers seemed like an obvious starting point. I had met many of them personally and most of the rest I knew by reputation.

Armed with my phonebook, I sat down and wrote introductory notes to all of the caterers in town. I used expensive stationary and was careful to use my best handwriting.

I received zero responses. None of them called. None of them stopped in my shop. None of them even sent a note telling me to take a hike.

Evelyn, my health inspector, dropped in for a monthly check of my bakery. She was a tough inspector. But I was a fanatic about following regulations and exceeding them where cleanliness and sanitation were concerned. It was natural that Evelyn and I became best friends. Our personal relationship never influenced our professional relationship.

After her inspection of my shop, Evelyn poured a cup of coffee and sat down to chat awhile. I told her about the introductory notes I had sent to all the area caterers and about my disappointment in receiving no replies.

She told me to relax; it was not a surprise. It was very unlikely that I would hear from any of those people until they got mad at the suppliers they were already patronizing. It was a matter of inertia. It was just easier to keep doing business with the same old people than find someone new and establish a rapport and good work relationship. You know, "If it ain't broke, don't fix it."

Swell! How do you create a working relationship with a caterer? Tricky question! You don't until they're upset with their current supplier. I had never thought about that possibility. Maybe that would never happen.

Evelyn looked at me out of the corner of her eye and said, "I can tell you something that will explode your business, but you may not want to hear it." Evelyn was always one to speak her mind, and we had become friends, so I knew it was difficult for her to hedge about telling me what she thought.

"Tell me what you're thinking," I said. "Let me be the judge of whether I'll buy into it or not."

Evelyn took a sip of coffee and looked me in the eye and said, "You need to start making wedding cakes."

Evelyn was hesitant to suggest I start offering wedding cakes because she knew how I felt about being in control of my shop. From our earlier conversations, she knew I absolutely did not ever want any employee to think they had me over the barrel. That meant that every job in my bakeshop had to be a job that I could perform myself. In case an assistant didn't show up for work one day or someone had to be terminated, I could step in and keep things on track.

I have Reynaud's disease. One of the effects of this condition is that I do not have great strength in my hands. That is why I had to give up the piano when I was a pre-teen-ager. No matter how determined I was or how diligently I practiced, I just was not good enough. And my hands would ache with pain. The best I'll ever be able to play is all right, and that's not well enough to satisfy the pianist that lives inside.

I had taken some beginner cake-decorating classes. I loved the design aspect of decorating. It excited me and opened new vistas in the landscape of my imagination. However, the physical act of squeezing bags of frosting to execute the designs I imagined was extremely difficult for me.

Since I *was* looking for a way to have my bakeshop expand and I valued Evelyn's judgment, I told Evelyn I would consider her advice. I told her I was not just putting her off. I really would explore the possibilities of adding cakes to my lineup of customer choices.

Something in the universe was at work. Two days later, a good customer who had bought lots and lots of my cookies called me. She sounded very agitated, and I soon found the reason. She said, "Oh, Evie, I have a friend who is really ill. Next week I'm afraid we may be celebrating her last birthday. If you made her birthday cake, it would make the day something she and her friends would cherish."

I explained to her that I was sympathetic with her problem, but I didn't do cakes. It sounded like something too special for me to experiment with. I tried to refer her to a very well-known bakery that did lots of cakes. She simply would not hear any refusals, reasons, or alibis. I had no choice but to create her a beautiful cake for her dying friend's last birthday.

In the following few weeks, I started receiving more requests for birthday cakes. I don't think any of the orders were related. It was as if everyone suddenly read the sign out front of my shop that said "Bakery" and decided that a bakery would bake cakes. My current customers figured since I made really good pies and cookies, I'd be able to make really good cakes as well!

I would design the cakes and bake them with my usual attention to style and quality. Fortunately, I had just hired a part-time employee who really liked to do cake decorating! She would handle the actual application of the design that I was physically unable to perform.

In what seemed like the blink of an eye, I was in the cake business. My business began to expand dramatically. Evelyn had been so right, and I will never forget my friend for her timely advice. It was such a blessing.

I hope you can see that my success has not come from any extraordinary abilities I possess. I'm certainly not trying to say, "Look what I did! Aren't I great?" I feel quite the contrary. This story, as most of the other episodes in this collection demonstrate, is simply to tell you that I have been blessed.

It began with smart, loving parents who took the time to teach me the value of honest, hard work. I have some skills, but every day I meet more skilled people who are not productive, not successful, and not happy. I have been lucky that events happened at exactly the right moment for me. But I've always remembered what some wise man once said, "Luck is the residue of hard work." When something broke my way, I was prepared and able to take advantage of that good luck.

I have continually been blessed by the appearance in my life of an incredible collection of people. Every time I found myself up against some snag, the door would open or the phone would ring. There would be a new friend-to-be with the answer to my difficulty. I always count these people a double blessing; they smooth my work life, and they enrich my life.

A powerful, loving, and nurturing God blesses me. I always have striven to include God in my business, my life, and all my decisions. When times have been hard and I could see absolutely no solution to some enormous problem, I would talk things over with God. The tools would be given to me, and this unbreakable problem would yield. I believe with all my heart that if God will lead you to it, God will lead you through it. But he will do it in *his* time.

Remember the carefully written introductory notes I had written to all the area caterers? I had not received a single reply. I was certainly disappointed. I moved on with developing a cake business within my bakeshop and didn't worry about caterer affiliation.

But just before closing time on a Saturday afternoon, a very well-dressed lady and her husband came into my shop. She introduced herself as Katie and her husband as George. By their demeanor, I could tell immediately that this couple was educated and successful. I always asked new people in my shop how it was that they thought to stop in to see me. Katie hesitated and actually blushed a little as she said, "Oh, Evie, I received your note last year, and I have just been so busy. I feel so guilty about never coming to see you before."

That's when I realized who this Katie was. Yes, she was one of the caterers I had written to. She went on to tell me she had just closed her very unique catering and café business. She was devoting more time to other activities, including her husband George, a very prominent physician in town.

I offered them seats at my dining room table and some complimentary cookies and coffee. George was tall and naturally slim. I had no idea that he had a killer sweet tooth. He grinned like a kid and was so glad he had come along for the visit.

Katie wanted to order a birthday cake. This Saturday ended wonderfully. I made a nice sale, acquired a good pair of customers and most importantly, from that time forward Katie, George, and I were great good friends.

Katie and George were very well connected, and the referrals they freely made to me of their business and personal friends helped grow my business and enlarge my clientele enormously.

Years later, when I was hospitalized with my disc problem, George would visit my hospital room every morning in his greens, even though he was not my physician. He was heading off to surgery but took the time to check on my progress. He advised Katie to have her friend, a fabulous massotherapist, look at me. That led to my back getting healed without surgery.

11

Old Friends Make New Harvests

God, good friends, and hard work, mixed with fortunate circumstances, had put Evie's in the cake business. My shop was acquiring a premium clientele and a solid reputation. However, I was not about to coast on my achievements. I could see the next phase of growth beckoning.

The wedding business twinkled on the horizon of my retail landscape like a shining star on a cloudless evening. Considering how I had resisted adding cakes to my bake-shop offerings, wedding cakes now seemed to be the key to firmly establishing myself in the retail world.

I believed my reasoning was sound. If I were to make just one magnificent wedding cake, a retail chain reaction would commence. I used very conservative numbers in my calculations. Say a gal named Jane had me create her wedding cake. That wedding would have one hundred guests. Half of them would be female. Half of them would be single and someday want a wedding cake as beautiful as Jane's. Jane's friends would throw her a bridal shower and would want a shower cake from the bakery that Jane had already chosen. If nature followed it's usual course, in a year, Jane's friends would be ordering a baby shower cake.

A few months later, a Christening cake would be needed. Birthday cakes roll around every year. All from one wedding cake!

To make all these plans come true, I needed to do only two things:

1. I had to get a wedding cake order from a bride-to-be.
2. I had to make that girl an Evie customer forever by delivering the most eye-popping, breath-taking, unforgettable cake.

I believed in my abilities enough to feel that I could handle number 2. To tackle number 1, I would need some big assistance from my friends and a sprinkling of good luck.

I figured when brides went in to arrange the details of their bridal flowers, they might want to know where they could get a beautiful and delicious wedding cake. So it was when I visited my old time friend, Jo, who owned a flower shop with her husband and family.

I told Jo what I needed and that I supposed that many brides had already made wedding cake plans by the time they came to see her, but if anyone was still looking for a good choice of wedding cakes, I would appreciate her referral. Wow! You bet Jo sent her referrals to me. I must tell you about her very first one. This all proves to be an example of the blessings God lays in front of you for the taking. My good friend Jo, the florist, was referring a bride to me for a wedding cake at the same time my friend Evelyn, the health inspector, was giving me some interesting advice.

And here's how it happened. The request was food first and a cake second. As I've mentioned before, my health inspector, Evelyn, became my business advisor. She had forty years experience seeing a variety of bakeries and restaurants from the inside. The stories and the lessons she had in her head were like gold. When she came to inspect my shop, she was all business, but after her work was done, she sat down for coffee and cookies, and we chatted. Her stories were priceless, and her advice was proving to be as well.

Evelyn had already prodded me into expanding into the cake business, and that was proving to be a huge success. Now Evelyn told me that I should do food too. I told her if people wanted breakfast or lunch, they could just go across the street to my brother's restaurant.

Evelyn said, "You need to do some simple catering." I argued that there was a caterer behind every bush and barn in the county. Plus, I reminded her that I was trying to get them to use my baked goods and send me referrals.

"Don't worry about those caterers," she said. "You bake better than they cater. I know you will create beautiful presentations too. They'll come around. You need to start doing some simple catering now." I respected Evelyn enough to tell her that I would think about it, and I meant it. Her advice had been right on point so far. I had to consider what she was telling me now.

Meanwhile, back at the flower shop, Jo was referring a bride named Chris to me for her wedding cake. Jo told her to call me for a wedding cake consultation appointment, and she did.

When Chris and I met, we hit it off immediately. This lady was an elegant combination of beauty and brains. She was a sales representative for one of the country's largest pharmaceutical companies and had a generous expense account.

After I designed her cake and wrote up the order, Chris asked me if I could help her when she called on her doctor's office business. I knew reps often took in goodies to doctors' offices to help open the doors and get a leg up on their competitors. Every pharmaceutical company had talented, well-funded representatives covering the same ground, and the competition was withering. Any advantage that could help get a rep past the front desk to steal a few minutes of the doctor's busy day to mention her latest medical breakthrough was a major victory.

Chris asked if I could do some lunches and some cookie platters. I recommended the best caterer in town for the lunches, and I'd do the cookies. I was pleased at the chance to show off my cookies to the town's best caterer. It could lead to lots of future collaboration. But Chris turned that down flat. She said, "Oh, Evie, I just know if you would handle this for me, it would be such a hit!" This is exactly what Evelyn had tried to tell me, but I didn't want to hear it. While I was considering it, Chris nailed me. She simply said, "Please do this for me, and do it in an Evie style."

I was hooked. A menu immediately came into my head. I knew I had some beautiful crystal bowls and silver platters wrapped up in boxes in the basement. I gave Chris a quick sketch of what I could do for her. She was delighted. I wrote up the order, and she paid for everything on the spot.

People often ask, "Where did you learn to cook and bake?" I always smile and give them the same answer, "I grew up in the two best kitchens a girl could have wished for: my pop's restaurant kitchen and my mom's at home. Are you kidding? Remember, I am Greek."

That night, I went downstairs and started my search for the items I wanted to use. I smiled, and my heart swelled.

It was like a Christmas morning. I had forgotten all of the lovely items that I had. An old part of my life was reopening, and it fit my plans for the future perfectly. I really had so much fun with this. It was truly a feel-good project.

I created a marvelous lunch and delivered it to the doctor's office along with a linen tablecloth and everything else that was needed. The doctor's office had a large kitchen/meeting room so the setup was easy.

I made friends with the receptionist and made sure that my flyers and business cards were tucked discreetly under one of my crystal bowls. I knew from some of the orders that came into my shop in the next few weeks that the office staff had found them.

Pharmaceutical reps have lots of competitors, but what is interesting is that so many of them are friends. There they would all be sitting in the waiting room to see the doctors and pitch their drugs. Chris told her competitor friends about me, and they were at her wedding too.

Soon, lots of pharmaceutical reps were calling me with their orders. I knew their companies sent them loads of marketing materials. They all acknowledged that they had tons of stuff they were dying to use but were tired of the same old presentations.

When they asked me to do something special to remember a doctor's birthday, I always inquired about which drugs they were promoting. I had oval-shaped cake pans and would frost the cakes off in a color that matched the color of the marketing materials they were using. We wrote the name of the product across the top as well as the birthday greeting. These became my logo cakes, and I was sure to be careful of copyright laws.

They often had packs of popcorn with their product name on them. I used to arrange them in with my individually wrapped cookies on platters.

I asked them if they had bakery boxes from their company. Their companies shipped their boxes with their products imprinted on them. The reps could buy donuts and put them in these boxes. Donuts? Are you kidding, when you could fill the boxes with Evie's cookies with the medicine's logo on each cookie? These reps really went nuts over this.

I had found a way for them to use their marketing goodies in a different way. And I didn't have to pay for any packaging. I used theirs. When these reps had special occasions in their own families, they called me. And so it just grew and grew.

Remember how I said the opportunity for continuing and expanding sales could grow from the capture of one wedding cake order? This is the type of harvest that keeps giving and giving.

12

Oh God, What Have I Done?
Part 2

Since I was full-time all the time at my bakery, I worked all the hours needed to fill the many cookie orders and the increasing number of cake orders I was receiving in my growing bakery. Believe me, I put in long hours.

Complicating the situation was the fact that the expanding number of cakes required a great deal more space. Several trays of cookies could be stacked in an efficient use of my limited space, but multilayered, iced, and decorated cakes simply couldn't be stacked. It was mentally and physically exhausting to constantly move and reorganize already baked items, as well as my equipment, in my small kitchen just to create space for another order. More and more cake orders were coming in, and they took up lots of room.

The situation came down to a simple (but scary) choice. In my current location, with every inch of the available space being used, I had already been forced to turn down orders and cease to grow. My brother had warned me about expanding. "You can always get bigger, but how do you get smaller?" That is how companies die.

Bob W., my banker, advised me I needed to sell my existing shop and move to a larger facility. He had told me years before that this would happen. Easy for him to say, but I was so afraid. So what do you do? Turn down orders and stay put, or take the leap and just do it? This was 1991, and the country was in a recession. I was really in a quandary as to what to do. Bob outlined my choices logically and let my good sense take over.

Finally, I sold my building of six and a half years and moved to a extremely large location just south of where I had been. Now I would be a tenant and not have the constant upkeep of my own building. This is what I thought anyhow.

Well-meaning friends thought I had lost my mind. Of course these same friends thought I had lost my mind six and a half years earlier when I left the bank to start this journey. I just told them, "It's a leap of faith. I've been blessed so far, and I believe it will only get better."

The proceeds from the sale of my little Dutch colonial were soon invested in remodeling the rooms that more than quadrupled my previous room size. The new space needed plumbing, electrical and gas lines, as well as serious carpenter's magic. I was really spending a lot of money. But this time, with my track record as a successful baker, I had no problem finding fantastic remodelers who did their jobs well and treated me with respect.

I moved out of my house and down the street. I opened the next day. Evie's Bakery had been down only one day. Planning, coordinating, and remodeling were all accomplished before we turned off the lights in the old shop. As I stood in the center of my new bakery before opening day, I had only one misgiving: why had I moved into such a huge place? It looked half empty. I hoped my customers wouldn't notice. Would you believe in just two years, we were once again bursting at the seams?

I had heard that in North Canton, there was a definite difference between North Main Street and South Main Street. I thought that was crazy. However, I soon discovered that North Main Street people never traveled to South Main Street (or vice versa). I still thought it was crazy, but that's the way it was.

When my customers called, I would remind them that I had moved. I gave them good housewife directions to my new location. The Hoover Company was on the square and was the dividing point for North Main Street and South Main Street. I carefully explained this to everyone that called. Many of my customers didn't live in North Canton, which added to the confusion.

Cell phones were just becoming popular, and many of my customers had them. You can imagine my amusement when I'd receive a frantic call from one of my customers. "Evie, where are you? I'm at your house, and nobody's here!"

Patiently, I would reassure them it was not a problem. The directions were simple enough that they didn't even have to write them down. "Just pull out of my old driveway and turn left onto North Main Street. Head south and pass the Hoover Company on the left. Come down ten more blocks, and I'll be on the left side of the street at the corner of Schneider and South Main Street. Just two lefts really: left onto Main Street, left into my parking lot. See you soon!" I had to repeat these directions over and over for a year!

It was reassuring to me that they just got in their cars and headed for Evie's. It was amazing. Some customers were in awe of the new shop, yet others would say, "I liked your little house better!"

13

I've Made It Bigger;
God, Help Me Make It Better

I spent the proceeds of the sale of my first building on remodeling costs on my new larger rental space. I had to install lots of plumbing lines to accommodate the gas and water. I had to set up my sinks and be sure electrical outlets were everywhere. I needed mixers, fridges, and so on. It truly is shocking to find out how expensive running electrical outlets down the length of a wall can be.

But since everything was torn up and being rebuilt, I was determined that this new space would have all of the workstations that I designed. They were glass enclosed and kept meticulous. It was truly a unique kitchen and receiving area.

The aromas of freshly baked goods would greet people as they came in. Foremost, it had to be welcoming and transport people into a calico grandma's kitchen.

So that's how I had used up the money I had acquired through the sale of my house/shop. It was well spent, *but* it was spent! Once again, since I didn't have sufficient working capital, I didn't have the luxury of working *rich*; I had to work *smart*. I needed to increase my sales, while not spending any money doing it.

When I was much younger, I used to envy the rich entrepreneurs, who could always just throw money at a problem and move on. But as I worked on making a go of my shop, in many ways I began to feel sorry for those guys with the big purses. They would never feel the satisfaction I had experienced when I made an idea work and my business grew because of it. I could sit bone-tired at night in my shop and know that it was all mine. At the risk of giving the cynics a good hoot, let me say, there are rewards and achievements more precious than money. Don't get me wrong. Money is nice too.

I kept thinking about the apple dumpling class at my old shop location. It had been great fun and had generated considerable business. What triggered the memories of that evening was when a recent customer mentioned that she was sorry for today's kids. They never get to see their mothers baking in their kitchens. Everything is pre-packaged and purchased at a grocery store or restaurant. I agreed with her and remembered my upbringing.

I knew scout troops and youth groups were always looking for free field trips. We had plenty of scouts in our area. So I got out the phonebook and starting making some calls. I called some local nursery schools too. Soon I had several afternoons booked with children coming to my new series of free cookie baking classes.

I had always enjoyed teaching. In banking, I was always selected to show other employees how to perform transactions or execute new procedures properly. I was constantly training my employees on the way we would do things at Evie's. Now I would teach baking to young children in my shop.

Pop always wanted me to be a teacher, and I knew he was proudly looking down on my efforts. In my mind, I could hear him in his adorable Greek-flavored version of English, "That's alright honeybunch. You do what you gotta do."

The children learned in a hands-on session how to make cutout dough, roll it out, cut it into various shapes, and place them on the cookie sheets. I assigned each child his or her own cookie sheet. I tinted egg yolks and painted the children's initials on their respective cookie sheets. That way, they were assured that they would end up with their own cookies. I baked their trays for them. After they were cooled, they frosted them.

I would not let them near the ovens. I made them stand back at a good distance, but since I had a large kitchen, their view was not blocked. They watched amazed as I explained the convection oven fan and how it made this oven bake faster than a regular oven.

I have to tell you. The very best students were the eight- to nine-year-old boys. They were so attentive, and they really loved their classes. They had never seen scratch baking before. I distributed a paper plate with a paper doily to each child. I instructed them to remove their decorated cookies from their cookie sheets and arrange them on their dishes. Then I laid clear plastic food wrap over the dishes so that they could be taken home.

Every one of those kids was proud as a peacock with their results. They made very sure their parents saw what they had made at Evie's.

14

A Memory of the Cake Man in the Window

I loved my shop and was excited by my chosen career. Now all I had to do was get customers into my establishment. I was depending on word of mouth carrying me once people tried my wares, but the problem was to get them in the door the first time.

Fortunately, a bakery draws people. There will always be a certain number of people who come into an unknown bakery simply because they love the mere idea of fresh baked goodies. But I needed to get more than that handful of devotees coming to Evie's. Keeping them coming back was a job I felt I would be up to.

I had heard that an ice cream parlor hosted children's birthday parties. I had also heard that a local roller skating rink did the same thing. I even knew a pizza chain was successful throwing birthday parties—hosted by a six-foot rodent, for crying out loud.

I have fond memories of the Arcade Market in downtown Canton. It was a unique assemblage of many vendors, including a produce market, butcher shop, grocery shop, and a bakery. They were all under the same roof, and people used to take the bus or drive downtown to shop there. They would stroll through the aisles with the various vendors presenting their offerings. The Arcade Market was very popular and quite successful until the suburban shopping centers came along.

My strongest and most wonderful memory of the Arcade Market is of the man who stood in the window, attired in a white chef jacket and hat, and decorated special occasion cakes. He seemed to work nonstop. It was like magic as he created such unbelievable beauty from his decorating bags and tools. I was awed by his skill. Whenever I was downtown with Mom, I would beg her to let me watch the cake man. She always put up a fuss about wasting time and so forth, but she always gave in. Mother would patiently wait beside me on the sidewalk as I was transported to a beautiful fairyland. It was a classic case of standing on the outside looking inside.

These memories never faded from my head, and I wondered if other children would be as fascinated with watching cake decorating as I had been. My son never showed any interest in my cake decorating; although in fairness I must confess, I had him tucked into bed when I did it.

And so in my best printing, I made some homemade signs announcing Saturday cake-decorating parties to be held at the bakery. I placed them on my counter, as well as hanging some up on my shop windows. When customers came to pick up their orders, I casually mentioned the Saturday parties in passing as well.

Soon, I was booking two parties every Saturday except for the months of November and December. I couldn't believe how many customers' children had birthdays in those months. You know what they did? They would book a half-a-year-to-my-birthday party! That way their children could have a birthday party at my shop and still fully enjoy all the parties and celebrating of the holidays.

These parties were not expensive to produce. I purchased brightly colored helium-filled balloons at our local grocery store and decorated the chairs around the table. I served a small lunch consisting of various sandwiches cut into different fun shapes, chips, and lemonade. I performed all the prep and clean-up work myself. It's a joke to tell how little I charged for these affairs. However, my goal was to build a customer base by getting people into the shop, not to turn a huge profit.

Parents were required to be there as well as some friends or family to help with the children. I had found out from the mother what flavor of cake to make and also some special favorites of our birthday guest of honor. Although I offered a full variety of cake flavors, the moms almost universally selected "one layer white, one layer chocolate." They weren't going to get too exotic and have unhappy guests at their kid's party!

The children's main table could accommodate twelve children. I set up a separate table for the parents on the side. After lunch, the tables were cleared, and my cake decorator brought in a large two-layer cake. After she was introduced, she began to frost off the cake. I told my eager audience that by the time we were finished, we would have a fantasy cake.

At my prompting, the eager children called for additions to the cake. At the beginning I would suggest surprises such as tiny teddy bears, ruffled swags, roses, dog paw prints, bunny rabbits, kitty cats, and so on. As my decorators executed the creation of the requested items, I explained how we made one decorating tip serve more than one purpose:

A grass tip can make fur on a teddy bear or rabbit.
A rose tip can also make a ruffled swag.
A writing tip can make dotted Swiss.

Soon all kinds of requests for fun additions were being shouted out by all the guests. One by one, my decorator quickly created the requested specialties on the growing work of art. Both of my decorators, Judy and Tara, were wonderful working with the children. Eventually the cake was completely covered. The only space left was on top, where "Happy Birthday" could be written artistically.

Then I would give the appropriate number of candles to the birthday child who would arrange them on top of the cake. I gave the mom the matches, and she would light the candles and make sure her child was able to blow out his candles.

I would make small strategic cuts around the cake and move these small cuts to serving dishes. I would then box the cake for the trip home to be viewed by the rest of the family members later that day.

As a finale, I would bring out a large tray with unfrosted, round cutout cookies. Each child had a cookie placed in front of him. I would ask if they had been watching Judy and Tara with their decorating. Then I produced tubes of colored frosting with attached tips for the children. Tara and Judy were there to assist them, and I told the children that they needed to share the colored tubes. Every one of them did. We never had fights over sharing the tubes or any other unpleasantness. The kids were always polite, and they loved the party. The parents were glad the kids were having such fun, and discipline was never an issue. Usually the mom was the parent who brought the child to the party, but the best workers and most fun to watch as they joined in decorating their cookies were the dads that were present. And *no one* had more fun doing it!

When the cookies were done, we provided lots of wet cleanup towels. Each child promptly turned in his decorating tools and went to work making his or her workstation at the table sparkling clean. Then I produced the clear plastic domed containers. Each cookie was carefully placed in a container, sealed, and wrapped with a balloon. The party ended as the children proudly took their cookie creations home to present to their parent.

I always provided a long table with a white linen tablecloth for a gift table. Sometimes, the birthday child opened the accumulated gifts at my shop; sometimes they didn't. That was their parent's decision.

Now how was I supposed to know that any of the mothers and friends attending the party was going to need a special cake the next year? And when this year's birthday guest had next year's birthday, you bet the cake had to be ordered from Evie's. Yes, these parties were extremely successful in creating future orders, as well as being a great fun time!

Everyone loves going to a birthday party. And I am no exception. It was with great sadness that I eventually had to discontinue these parties. My weekends became filled, as my wedding trade grew larger and larger.

15

Knowing When to Add Employees

As time passed and I began to see my clientele grow, my faith and courage grew in proportion. I started my bakery shop because I wanted to, and I thought I would be good at it.

Naturally I made some mistakes getting started, but the dream was true, and it kept shining before me through the long and lonely nights in my shop juggling bills, customers' orders, and available supplies.

I thought back to my father and how he just kept working in his kitchen. He never stopped. And I began to do what he did. My mind would flood with the beautiful melodies from our Greek Orthodox liturgy. I couldn't remember all the words because they were in Greek, and I didn't have my choir book, but the lovely melodies just filled my being as I went from task to task in my shop.

The Lord was always with me, and I realize now how the many wonderful people who came to me at Evie's were all his emissaries. Whether it was a persistent salesman or a new part-time worker or an unexpected new customer with a unique request, everyone who came to my shop must have been wearing a halo that I was too busy to notice.

As I came through trial after trial, I began to develop the mantra, "If the Lord brings you to it, the Lord will see you through it." Each adventure and each success were lessons in business and in faith.

*   *   *

A young college girl named Katie called me one day during her Easter break. She requested a job interview with me. I explained to her that I didn't have an opening, but she politely persisted. She said that she had heard about me and wanted to apply for a Christmas vacation job. I agreed to meet her in person. I welcomed her to come to see the shop and meet me. Who knows, at the least maybe she would send me some referrals. Well, I instantly liked her. She had grown up in her mother's kitchen and described some of the favorites she liked to make and bake. She was majoring in hotel management and had decided that working in a bakery would give her good future experience. Katie said, "Not to flatter you, but working for you, in your shop, would make spending my precious moments away from the college grind truly well spent." I *was* flattered, but I still didn't hire Katie. The next spring, she called me, and again I still didn't hire her.

Keep in mind that every holiday season I just worked myself like a crazy, possessed woman. I existed on two hours of sleep. I would drag myself home and throw myself into bed. Two hours later, I got up, showered, dressed, and trudged back into the shop. I just couldn't physically keep up with all the orders that were coming in. I was actually turning down some really good orders that came from referrals I had worked hard to get. Now it didn't make sense to sow so many seeds and then fail to reap the harvest.

But narrow, conventional thinking trapped me. I was following the nineteenth-century business philosophies of a very successful local company owner that had passed it on to me. He had told me, "If you can't be there watching them, then don't put on a third shift."

My employees were well trained, and with my background in banking, I made sure they were cross-trained too. Everybody knew how to bake the cakes, cookies, muffins, and small breads just in case I was conferring with a customer or involved in some other project that I couldn't break off.

This training was facilitated by the use of my step-by-step procedure book. Fortunately I had put it together for just this type of training. Here's how it came into being.

Donna, who was a good friend of my cousin Margaret, had a new business out of her home. It was word processing. I was eager to get some of my recipes organized and into a procedure book. One call to Donna, and she was on board.

All I had to do was write the recipes into the format that I wanted, and Donna would perform her magic on her keyboard. She brought me my first draft, and I was delighted by her suggestions and improvements to my original layout.

The entire idea was to enable my employees to look at this book and know how to proceed on their own. This book really did work, and I am sorry that I was never able to get more of my recipes to Donna to add to my book. When you read them, I'm sure you'll agree they are written to be understood easily. I've included recipes in this format at the end of some of the chapters.

Interestingly enough, she gave me her favorite coffee-cake recipe, which I did not put into my book either. She had typed the recipe on a piece of paper, and I taped it to a large index card. Donna said, "Try it, and I know you and your customer's will like it. This was a family recipe that had been handed down for years.

Oh my goodness, was it ever a hit. I used to bake it in a 9" × 13" pan and cut it into twenty-four to thirty-six pieces, place in paper cups, and arrange them on a platter with my muffins. One of my personal favorites that we used in the fall was my sister Joy's recipe for pumpkin muffins. These platters from Evie's replaced the traditional box of donuts at early business meetings. Sometimes I would scoop the batter into disposable foil pans. After baking and cooling, I would wrap and bow them for my customers to take as hostess gifts. As Valentine's Day approached, my purveyor supplied me with red foil hearts, and these heart-shaped coffee cakes really made a hit with my customers. "Always something different" was our motto, and these did it for me. Here are the recipes for Donna's coffeecake, Joyce's Arkansas apple coffeecake, and Joy's pumpkin muffins.

* * *

Coffeecake

Ingredients

- 1 stick softened salted sweet cream butter (1/2 cup)
- 1 cup sugar
- 2 eggs—set aside in a small bowl and beat. 1 cup sour cream or buttermilk—I always used sour cream which made a thicker batter.
- 1 1/8 teaspoon vanilla

1 teaspoon soda
1 1/2 teaspoons baking powder
2 cups flour

Directions

Use your electric mixer for this recipe. Put into mixer the butter and sugar, cream then add beaten eggs. Whirl around until mixed, then add sour cream. Mix again and add the vanilla. Whirl again, then add the soda, baking powder. Whirl, then add the flour. Whirl until mixed.

Smooth 1/2 of the batter into the prepared pan. Sprinkle 1/2 of the topping (see below for recipe), then smooth the remainder of the batter and sprinkle the remainder of the topping evenly over the top.

Topping

¾ cup sugar
2 tablespoon cinnamon
3/4 cup chopped nuts (optional- I did not use them)
3 tsp. cocoa

Bake in a regular oven at 375 degrees for 30–35 minutes.

In my convection oven, I baked this at 350 degrees about 20 minutes depending on what size and shape of pan I was using.

Reminder: If you are using foil disposable pans, place on a cookie sheet to bake. The heat will be better distributed if you place your foil pan on a cookie sheet.

* * *

My sister Joy called me and told me that she was excited about the recipe she had found in a newspaper. She had just made them for the first time, and they were absolutely delicious. She told me I had to have them in my shop. She wrote it down and mailed it to me.

As soon as the recipe arrived in my mail, I baked a batch. Joy was right. If anything, she had understated how fantastic they were.

As a time saver, I used to mix up the dry ingredients with the shortening ahead of time and place in an airtight container. I'd mix later on with the other ingredients and bake.

I never got this into my procedure book but had this on a large index card inserted into my procedure book.

I wrote it on a large index card with single batch, double batch, triple batch, and quadruple batch. I usually made the quad batches.

The following is for a single batch.

* * *

Sister Joy's Pumpkin Muffins

Ingredients

1 1/2 cups flour
1/2 cup sugar
2 teaspoons baking powder
I omit salt, but if you insist, the recipe did call for 3/4 teaspoon
1/2 teaspoon ground cinnamon
1/2 teaspoon ground nutmeg
1/4 cup shortening (I always use white Crisco)

Directions

Measure these ingredients into a large bowl and, using a pastry blender, chop/cut into the size of small peas. You can use two table knives and use a cutting motion until the desired consistency. If you don't have a pastry blender, invest in one. They really are so much easier to use than the other method.

Ingredients

Into a smaller bowl measure out the following:
1 egg
1/2 cup canned pumpkin
1/2 cup milk

Directions

Stir with a fork until mixed and then add to the dry mix as described above. Mix until moistened. If you want, you can stir in 1/2 cup raisins (per batch).

I learned to use a spray shortening such as Pam and lightly spray the bottoms of the muffin pans. If desired, a fine sprinkling of granulated sugar can be applied to the tops. What a delight when cooking spray came into the market.

What a time-saver. These muffins are not real sweet; I always felt that the tops should be sprinkled with sugar.

Fill the cups about 2/3 cups full.

Yield is 12 regular-sized muffins. These muffins are terrific in a petite size, and if you are using the small muffin pans, then the yield is 40.

In my convection oven, I baked them at 340 degrees for about 12 minutes. If you are using a regular oven, then you would adjust your temperature to about 400 degrees and bake for about 20 minutes.

* * *

I always liked a nice variety on my platters. So I need to tell you about Joyce's Arkansas apple coffeecake as well. She got this recipe from a friend at her church, who doesn't remember who gave it to her.

* * *

Arkansas Apple Coffeecake

Ingredients

> 3 cups of peeled and diced apples, set aside in large mixing bowl
> 2 1/2 cups flour
> 1 teaspoon baking soda
> 2 teaspoons baking powder
> 1 teaspoon cinnamon
> 2 cups white sugar
> 1 1/4 cups liquid vegetable oil
> 2 eggs
> 1 teaspoon vanilla

Directions

Add flour, soda, baking powder, cinnamon & white sugar to the apples in the large mixing bowl. Stir until blended.

Place the liquid oil, eggs, and vanilla into a separate bowl. Beat with a fork and add to the bowl of apples. Stir until combined. With a rubber spatula, scrape the mixture into greased pans. A 9" × 13" pan works well for this recipe. Bake at 350 degrees for about 25 minutes.

Various shapes and sizes can be used. Use your creativity. This coffeecake also is a pleaser when cut into squares, cupped with cupcake liners and arranged on a platter with muffins.

*   *   *

Now back to my story about Katie. For the third straight year, Katie called me. Before I could say no, she laid out a well-conceived plan that finally made me see the forest through the trees.

Katie said, "Evie, aren't you tired of turning down orders? You must be ready to trust me and let me work a third shift for you." She had really thought things out very well. "I could come in around ten p.m. or later and work until seven or eight a.m. I know you're working late, so there's no worry about giving me a key. Just let me know what you need done. Then you go home and get some sleep."

As usual, I worried about not enough orders coming in. This quickly proved to be absolutely ridiculous. Within a month, I was spanking myself because I had turned down orders that a third shift would have accommodated with ease.

Katie's proposal just made so much sense. She was home for spring break and wanted to set an appointment so that I could review recipes and procedures with her. I laughed. "Oh, you're going to remember all of this now for your Christmas employment?"

We met, and Katie looked as though she understood everything I explained to her. She spent the next day with me, and I felt comfortable with her quick training.

Everything I told her seemed fully absorbed. This girl was highly intelligent, and I could see her mother had given her very good training.

Fortunately, Katie's school term ended at Thanksgiving time, and she didn't have to return to college until the second week of January. How in the world had I survived before? Katie was such a fabulous person. She would come in at ten o'clock in the evening; I'd have everything written down for her. Then I'd verify that she could decipher my writing and knew exactly what I needed done.

She assured me that she knew what to do and shooed me out the door. Reluctantly, I left, but when I got home, I immediately went to sleep with this great sense of relief.

Still, I was back in the shop at five o'clock in the morning. Katie scolded me, but I felt better being there just to make sure. The next morning, I went in at six. On morning three, I went in at seven and realized that I was getting some much-needed rest.

By seven o'clock, Katie had everything done to perfection. Plus, she had every mixing bowl and cookie sheet she had used all washed. The kitchen was spotless, and I was ready to start with what I needed to do. All the cookie dough were in their containers, labeled and in the refrigerator. All the cookies that I needed to be baked were done and waiting for me. I could start arranging my assorted cookie platters. (Recipes at end of the chapter for pumpkin and old-fashioned sugar cookies.)

Katie worked two Christmas seasons for me before she graduated from college. She quickly received a big hotel job in Boston. I was happy for her but also melancholic to lose such a bright and talented worker who was also a friend.

I learned a valuable lesson. I know it was valuable because I paid a lot for it. The exhausting twenty-hour days and the turned-away business will never be recovered. And it was because I was afraid to try something new. "We've never done it that way" may have put the knife in the heart of more fledgling businesses than the taxman. If that is your business mantra, I strongly recommend you change it to "Dare to be different." You'll be glad you did!

Never ever lack confidence in yourself. Never ever let a fabulous employee *not* work for you. The dumbest thing I ever did was not hire Katie sooner. I never made that mistake again, but there was never another Katie.

As my business continued to grow, so did the need for additional employees. I had been very lucky to continually receive personnel referrals from business friends and customers, which always took care of my job openings. I had just let it be known that I was looking for someone, and a new hire was then recommended to me. I also called the local high schools and asked if they had a senior in their art classes that was interested in learning cake decorating. That's how I was able to recruit a very talented artist named Cary. All our decorating was done freehand. I never allowed the use of overhead projectors and image spraying. That's what the other bakeries did, and I simply didn't like the way it looked.

But when a vacancy developed this time, I had to resort to our local newspaper want ads. I had used wanted ads before and had met with disastrous results. That's why I was so eager to take on personnel who had been referred to me by their friends. My father always said, "Tell me who your friends are, and I know who you are!"

I needed someone to work one or two days a week to ice off cakes and prepare them for my decorators. When my decorators came in, they had already been prepped on the designs and were ready to start decorating. We found that it was a terrific time-saver to have my skilled decorators start right in working on already iced-off cakes. It was a simple plan, and it had worked well for us in the past.

The difficulty was I needed to find the person that was willing to only ice off cakes. And I needed them to come in around five o'clock in the morning when the freshly baked cakes were cool. Plus I only needed this person at the end of the week, which was my peak order time. My decorators started around 7:00 a.m., depending on the number of the day's orders and pickup times.

God sent me an angel in the form of a hard-working single mom with three children. She received no child support (I sure understood that) and desperately needed a part-time job. She worked full-time at a local in-store bakery of a very large grocery store chain and was not permitted to have a second job. She had two days off a week because she had to work weekends. She told me she was a very experienced baker as well as cake decorator.

I hired her immediately and reassured her that I would never snitch to her employer. Why would I? On her very first day with me, I realized that my prayers had been answered. Not only did she ice off cakes, but was a real whiz in rolling out cutouts! This was a job I always did myself.

Now I'm going to tell you about my last Christmas as a pastry chef, and I never told my angel about this. My husband, Ron, was with me at the shop early making lots and lots of cutout cookie dough. He asked how much he should make, and I just laughed. He made batch after batch of dough and kept up with my rolling out of trees, stars, and bells.

As soon as the cookies were cool enough, I left my rolling-out station and went to the frosting station to finish the cookies. Then when the frosting was set up, Ron would leave his mixer station and assembled platters for our orders.

I told Ron to keep making dough, and I would keep rolling out and frosting. When my angel came in, we would change workstations. Ron could go back to processing the orders, my angel could take over the dough making, rolling out, and baking, and I would just sit and keep frosting away.

When my angel arrived, I gave her the plan and told her how many trees, stars, and bells I still needed done. I went to my frosting station, and Ron took care of the orders for me. This was the last day of Christmas order pickups, December 24th, and I was absolutely exhausted.

As soon as it was eight o'clock, the phone started ringing with customers that apologized for not ordering before and just wondered if we had any extras. I had already warned everybody, "Don't even think about another order."

The time just flew as it always does when you are involved in a big project; it was time for my angel to go. Ron assured me that all was well. My angel had cleaned the kitchen for me (she was as meticulous as I am) and assured me that she had baked the entire cutouts supply that I needed.

All I had to do was just keep icing them off, and all Ron had to do was keep packaging. Then he started waiting on all the customers as they came in for their pickups. Oh yes, pick up times were from 1:00 p.m. to 4:00 p.m. Ha! I tried, but it just never worked out that way.

Gee, I just kept frosting, and the end was nowhere in sight. I asked Ron to do a recount of the orders. Ron is very smart, and when he came to me, he had a really strange look on his face; I knew we were in trouble.

"Oh no, I have been frosting for hours, do I have to start rolling out again? You'll have to start making dough because all of it has been rolled out. "No, I don't think our problem is that we need more cookies made."

"Oh good, then what's the big look on your face all about?" I asked.

Ron hesitantly told me, "I have counted and recounted, and somehow we have one thousand extra unfrosted trees on cookie sheets back on the cooling cart.

I could have just died! My angel was just so caught up with what she was doing she neglected to mark off her recap sheet of cookies needed. All morning, people were calling, and all morning we had turned down business!

I couldn't believe it. I looked at Ron and just started to laugh. He probably thought he was watching the beginning of a nervous breakdown.

"Okay, I'm going to just keep frosting these off, and then we'll box them and take them down to the Salvation Army. It's been a long time since I've taken them something.

I no sooner said that then the phone started ringing. I let Ron take the calls because I had so many cookies to frost off, and I knew how much time that was going to take. I needed to make more frosting, and I had not allowed for taking the time for that when I had planned my day.

Ron put the caller on hold and came to me laughing. He said the caller wanted to know if *by chance* we had any frosted cutouts. "Tell them I just have trees, and don't you dare tell them about stars or bells."

I listened as Ron said to them that we had some trees we could let them buy. Then I heard him say, "Sure, you could get three dozen." My jaw dropped open when I heard him say, "Okay, I can sell you six dozen. No, I am not kidding. You are lucky we have a few of the trees left!"

On and on it went. We even had a nervous grandmother call and ask if we had any unfrosted cookies. She had promised her grandchildren that they could come to her house and make Christmas cookies. She had the frosting made, had purchased lots of different colored sugars, but absolutely did not have the time to make the cookies.

"Sure," Ron replied. "I can box some trees for you. How many would you like? Yes, that's right, I'm afraid we only have trees. Sure, I can spare seven dozen for you. I'll get them boxed, and I'll see you in a few minutes."

Yes, God does perform miracles. Every one of those extra trees was sold in less than an hour. Somehow, God knew that I needed these extra sales because this was going to be my last Christmas. No one knew this besides Ron and me.

Since she's still working at that same grocery store bakery, I can't divulge her name. I'll just refer to her as "my angel," because God sent her to me when I needed someone with exactly her disposition and her skill set. One morning, soon after she arrived at my shop, she just started bawling. I immediately made her tell me what was troubling her. Her ancient used car had finally given up the ghost. I knew her car had been running on borrowed time, and I wasn't shocked that it had finally just died.

She told me that she had found a good used car, but the bank had refused to give the loan. The bank told her that she needed a cosigner. She was desperate. She had no family that would help her and had no idea what she was going to do.

I knew I had good credit. My parents worked hard and paid their bills before they ever thought of spending money on anything else. Expenses always came first and were paid on time. I was the same way.

I offered to be her cosigner. I told her that as soon as it was nine o'clock, she should call the bank for me. I would talk to them, and we would get this problem solved. She just stood there in stunned silence. I told her that this was not going to be a problem. She knew when I said something like that, I meant it, and she was instantly relieved.

Well, she got the loan and the new used car. I was so glad for her, and I was pleased that I had been able to help her. And that was the last I thought about the entire affair. I never worried about those payments because she gave me her word that they would be made on time. Apparently they were because I never heard from the bank, and she never mentioned her car finances again.

I just told her that someday she would need to pass it on. I explained to her that someday God would lead a single mother to her, and she must help that woman.

Many years later, I stopped in to see my angel at her work place and she said, "Hey, Evie, I passed it on." I guess I just looked at her with a "Huh?" expression on my face. I really had forgotten about the car loan.

She was bursting with happiness as she explained to me that recently she had gotten to know a single mother in desperate need. "Evie, I just told her not to worry and that I would help her with a solution to her problem. I also made her promise that she just had to pass it on someday.

I walked out of that store just feeling so good. My heart felt like it was the size of a basketball. I really had forgotten about the "pass it on" movement and reminded myself that this was something never again to be forgotten.

* * *

Pumpkin Cookies

My friend Cindy gave me these recipes. She popped into my shop one day and said, "Here, you have got to try these." I did, and they became regular offerings to my customers. They arrange on an assorted platter beautifully and do freeze well too. I do not know the origins of these recipes.

Ingredients for a single batch of pumpkin cookies (Yield: depending on the size of scoop you use, lots!)

1 cup (white) Crisco
1 cup white granulated sugar
1 cup of canned pumpkin (if you buy a 15-ounce can, then make a double batch and use the entire can. Be careful. Do not use the canned pumpkin that already has spices in it)
1 egg
1 ½ cups of chopped nuts or raisins (optional)
1 teaspoon cinnamon
½ teaspoon ground ginger
¼ teaspoon ground cloves
1 teaspoon soda
2 cups flour

Into an electric mixer bowl, place Crisco and sugar, beat, then add pumpkin and egg. Beat again until thoroughly mixed. Don't forget to scrape down your bowl with a rubber spatula.

Add the cinnamon, cloves, soda, and mix until blended.

Add the flour and mix thoroughly.

Scrape into a bowl, cover, and refrigerate until batter is in a scooping consistency. Bake at 350 degrees on ungreased cookie sheets for 6 minutes, alternate the cookie sheets, then bake for an additional 4 minutes or so until the bottoms are light brown and the tops when touched are not depressed. Scrape cookies with metal spatula; allow them to cool on cookie sheet; then frost with my buttercream frosting. This is a great cookie to freeze.

16

Fake Cakes Are the Real Deal

I kept finding new reasons to be pleased with my new location. It had lots of windows and was at the end of a one-story building. Plus I was situated on the corner of a very busy intersection. When cars stopped at the light, the drivers naturally turned their heads toward the massive picture windows.

I then had an idea; I should make a couple of elegant sample cakes for display. People always raved about how beautiful my cakes were, so I thought if they saw a sample of my cakes as they entered my shop, they might be encouraged to order one for themselves. I couldn't make real sample cakes because they wouldn't last, and in no time, they would look dreadful. So I decided to make some sample cakes out of Styrofoam. It would be expensive and not easy to make. By this time, my confidence had grown, so I knew my new displays would be valuable tools.

No matter the type of business, there are slow times. Do you cut back on the employee's hours, or do you have enough courage to work on displays to create future sales? Spending money on payroll on Tuesdays and Wednesdays for window displays was the correct decision.

On some slow Tuesdays and Wednesdays, I would just tell the girls, "I'm running down to Flower Factory to get some sprigs of pearls. I'll be back." While I was in the store, I would also purchase some Styrofoam circles.

Icing off Styrofoam circles and trying to convert them into decorator sales pieces is no piece of cake. The stuff is scratchy and gives off yucky debris.

I would bring in the bags of stuff and announce that the cake we had just done the week before for Mrs. Whoever needed to be reproduced as a Styrofoam cake for a window display.

The girls would roll their eyes and give me looks, but they knew how committed I was to this, so they would heave huge sighs of resignation and began working. They already had their written instructions and just needed to confirm with me what was to be done. Piece of pie! Or should I say, piece of cake!

I added interest to the window displays by elevating the cakes on glass blocks, camouflaging them with yards of tulle softly draped upwards and around or by placing them on top of pedestal cake stands. My dear friend Jo from Canton Flower taught me how to drape tulle or colored satin around the bottoms of the cakes.

The Styrofoam displays certainly did pay for themselves. Customers would walk in, go over to a display, and say, "That's exactly what I want."

I had designed a cascading design using a lily tip. My inspiration was from the headpiece of one of my bridal customers. When Zahra's mother came in to order her daughter's wedding cake, she brought a picture of Zahra's headpiece. Of course, I described with my "Greek talking hands" the cascade that would almost match. I translated that cascade into her wedding cake. When the cake was finished, Zahra and her mother were ecstatic. So was I! The cake had turned out even better than I had described to them. More times than I care to remember, I tossed and turned in my bed, worrying if my design would work and if the bride, her family, and her guests would like the result of my efforts. I never had a complaint in that department, but I still worried with each order. I would always stand back and admire the finished cake. Then I would get my decorator and say, "Okay, let's look at this and admire what we've done here."

I was always so proud of my decorators. I truly do not know how they put up with me sometimes. I constantly made them do decorating that they had never done before—actually, it was often decorating that *no one* had ever done before! They were continually frustrated by my confidence in them that they could go beyond what they thought was their limits of creativity!

The week after the wedding of the lovely lady named Zahra, the lovely Styrofoam cake named Zahra went on display in the front window of my shop where she brought in lots and lots of orders.

Those beautiful three words, "I want that," just kept working. So we added more and more Styrofoam cakes to showcase our unique talents. Eventually our windows were filled with cakes like Zahra and many others. "Pink and Pretty" sat on the top of the antique sideboard next to my grandmother's table. I am not bragging, but my shop was just so lovely.

What I did not realize was the response from some of the local interior decorators in town. They worked with builders on decorating their model homes. One of these interior decorators came into my shop, not to buy a cake, but to ask a special favor.

I was asked to make one of my Styrofoam cakes for helping create the ambience in the master suite staged to illustrate an elegant breakfast. The breakfast tray was placed on the bed, with a Styrofoam model of one of my cakes surrounded by expensive linen, china, and silver.

I received another happy surprise. One day a lovely lady came in and introduced herself to me as the manager of the bridal registry department at the largest department store in our area. She asked if I'd do her a favor. I told her, "Sure. How can I help you?" She immediately turned and pointed to one of the small decorated model cakes in my window. She wanted to know if she could purchase one to display in her department. She assured me she would have it under a clear, acrylic dome so that it wouldn't be touched or damaged. The following week, I personally delivered it to her. She proudly showed me how she had the dome already prepared. She even had a beautifully framed sign identifying the cake as an "Evie cake."

It's been said, "If you build it, they will come." I say, "If they see it, they will order it." This got me to thinking. My referrals needed to come from other businesses that were in the wedding business too.

I always asked my brides who their florists were so if they wanted them to do floral treatments on their cakes, I would need to call them to coordinate our joint efforts. I would also ask them who their photographer was and request a picture for my album. I got to know these florists and photographers because of my customers. I wanted their referrals.

I once heard that grocery stores have limited shelf space and vendors are carefully allocated shelf space according to what the store can spare. I knew what it was like not having room for everything too. Considering this, on a slow Tuesday or Wednesday, I made calls to florists and photographers that I knew had seen my wedding cakes. Upon arrival, I surveyed their shop and calculated their space. Then I made my proposal. To the florists that I did call on, I asked if I could place a small or large decorated wedding cake in their shop, and they could decorate it with their silk flowers. This way, brides would be inspired to have their floral treatments on their wedding cakes instead of my frosting flowers. This was a win-win for both of us. Of course, I had my business cards on the table. I was successful in doing this with three local florists. Yes, my decorators were paid to create these Styrofoam cakes, and I delivered them.

I did the same thing with photographers—I set up a cake table in their studio. Fortunately for me, they would provide the table, so I didn't have to haul one there. I always offered to bring my own tablecloth, which they felt was helpful. I set up my wedding cake using silk flowers, making sure my business cards were in front of the cake on the table. My display added an air of wedding festivities to their wedding consultations and certainly gave me a referral for another wedding cake. I always was mindful of their room space. A small table was sufficient for my display purposes.

Remember how I told you that I absolutely loved fabrics? Designing in another medium and being among wedding gowns was such a privilege. I always thought that an ideal vacation day would be spent just wandering aimlessly through a bridal salon, looking and touching and admiring bridal gowns all day. I decided to do that, and make a business connection at the same time.

I got to know Doreen because of my dear friend Kate. One day, I thought it would be a good idea to get out of the shop and go up to see Doreen at her new bridal shop in Hartville, a small town just north of me. Doreen's shop was so beautiful, and we became good business friends. She was not only a highly talented seamstress but was trained in fabric restoration. Christu Bridals was south of me in Canton. I have a deep love for this family. I thought I had better go down to say hello to them as well. They both told me about upcoming trunk shows. I had heard somewhere about trunk shows, but I didn't really give the concept much thought. Both of them periodically had them, and both told me I was invited to participate.

This was what I did for the bridal houses. By now I had found many uses for those clear clamshell containers. I made lots of cupcakes with a full buttercream rose on top. I placed two of these cupcakes adjacent to each other in a package and then wrapped them in white tulle ribbon and tied a bow on top and taped my business card to the bottom. (I didn't want to spoil my pretty presentation by sticking the card on top.)

I delivered the cupcakes to the respective shops, with my compliments, when they were having their shows. They handed them out as appreciation gifts to the customers that attended. This cost me payroll and materials, but the good will that was created was priceless!

One business can help another, and what better advertising for me than a perspective customer tasting my product. Were the owners and employees of these shops my customers? Of course they were. Did they have special occasions occurring in their families, and did they call me for their orders? Of course they did!

There is a cost of doing business that the wise business owner embraces. My philosophy was always to do *cost-effective marketing*, and this proved to be a good example.

I always asked customers how it was that they had called me. Soon, I received the same response over and over, "Well, everybody I know just said to call you."

17

You Can't Bake a Cake Till You Design It

I have never understood how a custom-order business could be closed on Monday. That was our planning day. All final counts from brides for the upcoming weekend had to be confirmed. Their caterers and florists had to be called so that we could coordinate the delivery and setup times of our cakes.

Most importantly, Monday was the day when I sat down with my decorators and we decided how to decorate each tier. Everything was decided upon and written down. My unwritten (but unbreakable) rule was to never to have two tiers of a cake decorated the same. I made life a lot harder on myself by never yielding on this point, but it was an immense source of personal pride for me. Plus, one of the things that made a wedding cake from Evie's so sought after was it always had a unique look.

Karen, my first cake decorator, was an absolute gem. She would have been with me until I closed my shop if she hadn't gone off to college to become a nurse. She was the creator of the extremely popular Evie's "Pink and Pretty" design.

When I was a little girl, my mother made all my clothes. I loved to accompany Mom to her favorite fabric store. There, I was transported to a wonderland of bolts of fabric. How I loved the colors and textures. While Mom was looking at fabrics, so was I.

One of my most cherished dresses was the pink-dotted Swiss dress my mother made me for my cousin Joanne's wedding. Mother even made a purse to match. That's when my love for dotted Swiss was established. Since then, it's been my favorite material.

I asked my decorator, Karen, if she was familiar with dotted Swiss fabric. She said she was and indicated she loved it too. We decided to create a cake design with dotted Swiss fabric as our inspiration. Step one would be to place dots on our iced-off cake. Right out of the gate, we had our hands full. Placing dots on a freshly iced cake is very difficult. It requires scads of patience and skill to get the dots evenly placed. When the dots had set up, we then had to lightly tap on them to knock the tips off. We were bad girls when we started, referring to these tips as a small part of a woman's chest, but the naughty nickname stuck. Thus, "Pink and Pretty," with lots of ruffled swags and dots was born.

The frosted cake color and the color of the dots could be the same color or different colors, depending on the decoration for the top of the cake. Color combination was always a prime consideration when taking the customer's order.

I always enjoyed it when customers came in personally to place their new orders. Each cake order was inspired by the customers' theme, colors being used, the interest of the recipient, and the occasion. A fiftieth anniversary would be easy. People usually wanted the color of gold, and so the theme evolved from this color.

Children's birthday cakes were difficult because the parent would always bring in a copyrighted napkin and say, "This is exactly what we want." I would smile and turn the napkin over to show them the little *c* on the napkin. I would then explain what that meant and the restrictions it placed on the napkin design's use. Instead, I suggested that we could design a cake that captured the colors and the theme of the napkin.

When the groom's cake was themed to his profession or his alma mater, I insisted on a letter from his school allowing me to duplicate his alma mater or the emblem of his profession. I received letters from The Ohio State Dentistry School and Penn State just to mention a few. You bet I hung them up for display. This gave customers some idea of the lengths we would go to in order to satisfy their wishes.

When a mother wondered, "Could you make a treasure chest cake?" or "Could you make a train cake?" "How about a baby carriage?" I would promptly shift into full gear. I talked with my Greek hands, describing how the cake we could create would perfectly accomplish what they wanted. The customer walked out the door excited, and I was left to face my decorators with the project I had just promised. My decorators knew one response was absolutely unacceptable: "But we've never done that before." That was exactly the point. We were constantly adding new designs to our file.

Karen always told me that someday I should publish a book illustrating my designs. During my last few years, I had Tara sketch the cake designs we were doing and make notations of the tips that we used. We were very creative at getting special results from a tip, other than what the tip was created to do. These patterns resemble the color charts on embroidery directions. I pray someday Karen, Tara, Cary, and I can compile a book that will be the definitive cake design album.

It made it easier to look at prior designs and incorporate changes to accommodate the needs of the current customer. Each design was given the name of the customer for which it was originally created. When I told my decorators, "Let's do Zahra," they knew just what I was talking about.

We had our procedures. There's that bank training again. Once Thursday and Friday came, I did not want to have to stop to answer any questions unless absolutely necessary. Often, I would start baking at one o'clock in the morning, and the kitchen and decorators' stations would be filled with cooling cakes on their racks, tagged with customers name, size, and flavor. When the decorators came in, they knew to sign in, wash up, and begin icing off or decorating those cakes.

18

Evelyn, You Were So Right

My good friend, Evelyn Walther, the health inspector, told me to start doing wedding cakes so that I could increase my business. What she didn't tell me is a key marketing lesson I was glad I learned when I took on the world of brides and wedding cakes at Evelyn's urging.

All brides have friends that are going to be in their wedding and are probably going to be getting married in the near future. Everyone of these friends asks the bride when they're ready to start planning their wedding, "Who did your wedding cake"?

Without fail, when a customer placed an order, I always asked, "How is it that you decided to call me? Do I know you? Have you ever placed an order with me before?" My employees also were instructed to find out the source of our referrals on every order they took.

So this is how I know the following to be true: Lots of orders would stream in from the order of one wedding cake. *Lots of orders!* Future brides would universally reply, "Oh, I was in Susie Q's wedding, and I asked her where she got her cake. She said, 'Oh, just call Evie.'"

Often, the bridal attendants couldn't remember what their friend's cake looked like. But I must admit others described the cake in infinite detail by decoration and flavor.

Brides are given bridal showers. That cake is always ordered from where the bride has ordered her wedding cake. Here's an idea that I came up with for my niece Stephanie's shower. I had a plan for doing something really different. When I attended the meeting of the hostesses that were planning the event, I presented my idea. The shower was a luncheon with about eighty people attending. That's the way my family does things.

I proposed that I put a cake in the center of each table. Combining the centerpiece and the dessert would save expense. The committee had estimated that about eight tables, each seating ten guests would be required for the luncheon.

This is what I did. I made a double six-inch round cake and decorated it with ruffled swags and Cornelia lace down into the swags. I placed the cake on a six-inch glass block in the center of the table. Then I puffed up two yards of white tulle. I wrapped the glass block inside the tulle with a linen napkin and draped the tulle around the block. Another one of the hostesses offered to buy silk roses so that I could tuck them into the folds randomly around the tulle. The block was completely hidden, and the cake floated in the center of the table on a cloud of tulle.

Since a hostess would be seated at each table, I suggested that at the end of the meal, each hostess take the cake at her table back to a dessert prep table. The table would have dessert dishes, forks, and napkins. I requested that each hostess cut her cake, get the pieces onto the plates, and serve them back at her table, along with the forks and napkins. I brought along a cake box for any leftover cake. I placed the leftovers into the box and presented it to the bride's mother to take home.

I had instructed the hostesses to cut the cakes into sixteen wedding cuts so that there would be leftovers. The cuts were not small because I baked thick layers. I also had made and arranged cookie platters, which were taken to each table.

The shower guests were surprised, and this very novel dessert centerpiece was a hit. How could it not be a hit? Imagine a centerpiece that was both beautiful and yummy! I sold this idea successfully many times to my future brides who knew they were going to be given a shower.

Wedding cake orders are often placed a year in advance. Can you imagine the many occasions that occur in the bride's family in that year leading to the wedding? For instance, just consider a family's many birthdays for the mom, dad, grandma, grandpa, sister, brother, nieces, and nephews. All of these orders came about because of a wedding cake that hadn't even been baked yet!

Let's add this all up. I made the bridal shower cake, then the wedding cake, then the baby shower cake, and then the first birthday cake. Let's not forget the bride's extended family and their special occasions. "Just go see Evie."

I got to grow with my adopted family of customers, and they remained loyal to me. Now you see why it was such a fantastic idea for me to do wedding cakes, and I am forever grateful to my health inspector for telling me to do it.

19

After the Cakes Are Eaten, the Customers Return for More

It was after I moved my shop to the new location that my wedding cake business really began to take off. There were several reasons for this. First, I didn't have to turn down business because now I had the room to do it. I had added staff and could afford to use some of my time to develop this area of my business. I visited florists, photographers, and wedding gown shops to establish connections with people already working with prospective brides.

Many times, a future bride would have pictures taken of herself in her gown at the bridal house so that she could take these to the florist to assist as a tool in designing her bridal bouquet. I began to ask each bride to bring her pictures to me so that I could design her wedding cake to coordinate with her gown. Wow, did that ever go over well!

Fortunately, Tara, a superbly talented decorator on my staff, had sketching skills. When the bride would come in for her cake consultation and had brought her pictures, I would ask Tara to join us with her sketchpad so we could work on a design for our bride.

As I talked with my hands, Tara would sketch. The development of the design was collaboration with the bride, her mother, Tara, and myself. All the while, Tara would just keep drawing. We were unique. Absolutely no one around made a wedding cake to look like the bride's wedding gown. As an additional benefit to the proud bride, the new cake design was named after her.

With my love of fabrics and laces, I was in my glory looking at these bridal gowns, which guided my designing. My dear aunt Sophie always told me I could be a fashion designer, but I never thought I had that much talent. I always felt that Aunt Sophie was sitting in at my consultations, smiling proudly at me.

Amazingly, I soon found myself with more bridal referrals and business that I could handle. You can only accommodate so many weddings in one weekend. I reluctantly had to start turning down orders. That's why it was so comforting to have wedding cake orders placed a year in advance. When a particular date was full, we had to say, "I'm sorry, but we can't handle your request on that date."

Only once in my memory did we avoid the weekend crush when scheduling wedding cakes. An established customer excitedly called to let me know she was getting married. She was calling with a two month's notice for a Friday night. The wedding was going to be low key. After work, they were going to a judge's office to get married, then go across the street to a very nice restaurant to celebrate with immediate family and friends. The only extravagance was that the cake had to be an Evie cake.

I was booked solid and could not take her order. Jokingly, I said to her, "Now, if your wedding was on a Wednesday night, I could take your order."

She said, "I'll call you back." Within ten minutes, my phone rang; it was the bride-to-be. "I'll do it! I changed everything to Wednesday. *Now* can I get an Evie wedding cake?"

I happily replied, "Absolutely. Now let's talk flavor and design."

When all the details had been taken care of, she said, "I'll have my friend come in and pick up the cake."

I said, "Oh, no. We will gladly deliver it for you." And so we did. This cake was as carefully prepared, delivered, and setup as any cake that ever came from Evie's Bakery.

From a cash flow standpoint, this was a reassuring situation. Any business owner will tell you that if they could manage one element of their business better, it would be determining peak times and trying to estimate the cash flow. That is exactly what booking wedding cakes a year in advance did for my shop.

The last week of November and all of December was just too hectic for even one wedding booking. I did do one Thanksgiving weekend wedding and nearly lost my mind trying to get caught up with the incredible pace of business in December. The firm rule was this: pre-Christmas weddings were never booked.

I started to close for a break between Christmas and the first week into January. I did turn down some orders so that I could keep the shop closed and hop a plane out to see my sister and her family out west.

20

If They See It, They Will Buy It

Accommodating my customers' requests was the essence of my business. Many times, customers walked in the door and said, "I want to order a cake. Do you have any pictures?" I never wanted to admit that I didn't have a camera. Come on, I'm a Greek girl who talked with her hands and quickly designed a cake just for them.

Soon customers were bringing me pictures of the cakes they had ordered so I started an album. They stood and watched me as I placed their cake's photo into this new album. They could not have been more proud if their kid had just won the academy award. This *free* album was the very best marketing tool that I had! Why hadn't I thought of this before?

It was always such a compliment when someone like Niki came to me for an order. Niki was a known gourmet cook and baker. I was developing a good reputation, but I was not accustomed to the notoriety yet, so celebrities like Niki impressed me a great deal.

Niki had never been in my shop before nor had she ever ordered anything from me, so when she called to set up an appointment to come and see me about her daughter Sherry's wedding, I was really excited.

She wanted me to do the cake, but with one condition. Sherry's absolute favorite was her mom's carrot cake, and Niki wanted to bring her recipe with her.

I reluctantly agreed because I already had a fantastic carrot cake recipe that Joyce had given to me. Keep in mind that I had a big old Blodgett convection oven that required special handling. I had already experimented with all my recipes in the Blodgett and adjusted the baking temperatures and times to the convection oven's requirements. New recipes meant time-consuming experiments.

Sherry lived out of town and wanted to come home for her wedding and reception. As so often happens with out-of-town brides that grew up in our area, their mothers interviewed me and all of the other wedding professionals that would be working on the wedding. I met with Niki, and she really liked my shop and was very complimentary.

At my wedding interviews, I always served my client coffee and a variety of flavors of cupcakes. Not only did I feel this practice set a gracious tone for our discussions, it also gave my client an opportunity to sample the different flavors.

I asked about Sherry's tastes. Niki reminded me that she had been at my niece's wedding and really loved all the ruffled swags and sprigs of pearls on her cakes.

"Evie, I trust how you'll decorate Sherry's cake, and I know you'll make it beautiful. I only have one request. You use my recipe. I want all the layers in carrot cake." I bravely responded to Niki by saying that I had a really good recipe, but if hers was better, I would gladly use hers.

Being the highly accomplished and very efficient lady that she was, she dropped off her recipe the next day. I assured her that I would bake a batch within the next few days and call her with my opinion. This recipe had a lot of eggs and liquid oil and tons of shredded carrots. Because of the oil, I knew it would take longer to bake than my other recipe.

Oh, was Niki ever right! That cake was just heavenly! Her order was composed of a lot of servings, and I peeled and shredded carrots all day just to prep for this order. It was worth it!

The groom hated carrot cake and wanted some chocolate. Now that was a request I could certainly understand. He just wanted good old buttery chocolate, so I made a large two-tiered, heart-shaped groom's cake for him. It was a chocolate cake with chocolate frosting. I placed this groom's cake to the side of the main cake. I made another decorated heart cake to go on the other side to balance the presentation. This cake was made out of carrot and was frosted off in my vanilla buttercream.

Fortunately, I knew their wedding photographer. He was one of the top photographers in town. I called him and asked him if he would take a picture of this cake on the cake table for me. I placed the order and asked him to also frame it.

A few weeks went by, and Joe stopped in with my framed picture. It was pricey, but it was so beautiful that I was absolutely thrilled with it. I immediately named it Sherry's Cake. I knew the perfect spot for it. When customers came in, there was no way they could not see it. I hung it on the wall opposite the front door. It really knocked your eyes out when you came into my shop.

More often than not, brides would walk over to the picture and say, "I just want that." What was tricky was that often they only needed a third of the servings. I politely explained, talked sizes with my Greek-girl hands, and did a fast redesign. (Carrot cake recipe at the end of the chapter.)

* * *

Nicky's Carrot Cake Recipe

I do not know where she got this recipe, but it is fantastic. You'll agree with me when you taste it. Remember my hint about having prepared grated carrots in the freezer?

1 1/4 batches will yield 2 8-inch round baking pans.

Be careful. This batter will rise during baking. Do not try to make thick layers; due to all of the oil in the batter, there is a longer-than-usual baking time.

This recipe is for one full batch.

Ingredients

    2 cups white granulated sugar
    4 eggs
    1 ½ cups of vegetable oil
    2 teaspoons vanilla
    2 teaspoons baking soda
    2 teaspoons cinnamon
    3 cups shredded carrots
    2 cups flour

By hand, place into a large mixing bowl the sugar and eggs, then beat with a large fork.

Add oil, mix, then add vanilla, soda, and cinnamon, blend thoroughly. Add the carrots, mix, then add the flour and mix until blended.

Pour into greased and floured cake pans.

Bake at 350 degrees for 30 minutes until toothpick inserted into middle comes out clean. Remove from oven and place on cooling wire rack. Remember my trick to reduce a humped-up cake: place another cake rack on top. Run a knife around the top edge and inside of pan. Cool for 10 minutes, then flip over to remove cake pan. Cool completely. Frost with my homemade buttercream frosting. You could use a cream cheese frosting, but I never did. I would have worried about refrigeration with that type of frosting. Enjoy, and I now will say thanks again for a great client for insisting that I use her recipe and she was so right.

21

Grains of Sands Turn into a Hailstorm of Rocks

By now you know that many of my customers became my friends. You have also seen how I utilized my marketing skills to create a business from scratch.

I now must tell you about my new friend Elaine and her husband, Dick, who was an engineer. Elaine worked for the telephone company, which had undergone several mergers and acquisitions. Due to these changes, she had to drive up to Akron and did not like the drive. What made it even worse was that she didn't like a lot of her new fellow employees. However, she was in a supervisory position, so she couldn't show her dislike of anyone!

Interestingly enough, it was Dick that called for their first order, which was a small decorated cake for Elaine's birthday. There was just the two of them because the few relatives that they had lived out of town. They did not have any children.

It happened so many times that the recipient of a birthday cake would personally stop in to thank me for making their birthday a more festive occasion because they were given an Evie cake.

Elaine soon realized that I worked all kinds of crazy hours and inquired if I went to church on Sunday mornings. I confessed to her that I could not do that any longer. I did miss attending church and singing in my choir. Sunday mornings were spent paying bills and preparing them for my accountant. After this paperwork was done, I would start in the kitchen and get cookie dough made and into the refrigerator for the next day's baking.

You had to know Elaine's character. She was a nervous, generous, "you can't say no to" type of person. She told me that when she didn't have to work on a Saturday or Sunday, she and Dick would get in the car and drive to discover a new adventure. She described many of the places they had visited, and these times certainly did sound like a lot of fun.

I have to tell you that Elaine often rapped on the front door of my shop around 5:30 a.m. before heading up to her office. Dick had restricted her coffee, and she knew my coffee pot was always on for my friends.

One morning, I heard the tapping of her car key on my front door, and she burst into the shop with this exclamation, "Evie, this Sunday, Dick and I are picking you up, and I have no clue where we're going, but all I know is that you are included, and don't even try to tell me how much work you have or offer up any other excuses to me. That's all you ever do, work. You need to get out of here."

I immediately felt guilty. If I had time to go out with Elaine and Dick, then I should go to church. I told this to Elaine, and she could not believe me. She again repeated her offer and said they would pick me up this coming Sunday at the shop at eight o'clock in the morning. She also informed me that I was not to bring any money because they were buying lunch except she didn't know where. We spent that Sunday together and had great fun.

A few weeks later, Elaine asked, "Do you have a slow day in the week? If it is Tuesday, that would work out good because I have Tuesday off." Sometimes, if she had work emergencies that she had to cover over the weekend, she was given a day off during the week.

I reviewed my next week's order file and determined that I probably could pull this off. I had dependable, cross-trained employees that were good at following my instructions, so I figured this would be okay.

That Tuesday, I must have started in the shop by one o'clock in the morning so that I could leave at eight o'clock with Elaine. I had everything done so my employees could take over for the rest of the day. I didn't have a cell phone. Neither did Elaine. How she howled that I was such a worrywart.

I couldn't give my employees my itinerary because I didn't have one. I just trusted that everything would be okay, and it was. We returned after five that night and I raced into the shop checking to "just make sure." Everything was in order, and I really was proud of my employees. I had had such a good time. We drove into southern Ohio and ate lunch at a restored historic inn. The food was fantastic. Since it was spring, Elaine guided me to a public garden and a famous pottery in Zanesville. I insisted on driving and burning my gas. The whole time, Elaine kept asking, "Do you always drive the speed limit? Can't you speed it up?"

The next week, Elaine pulled her usual "need a quick cup of coffee" line and gave me a small bag and just said, "I don't know if you have ever seen this, but I think you might enjoy reading it." And out the door she went.

I opened the bag and found a beautiful piece titled *Footprints*. I had never seen this, and as I read and reread this little passage, the tears just poured down my face, and I could not stop crying. I must have cried for at least thirty minutes. Due to copyright laws I cannot reprint this for you. Please, at your earliest convenience, buy this at any religious store.

How absolutely arrogant of me to think that I had been so strong to get through all of the rough spots that I had had to endure. Just who did I think I was anyways! Yes, I had come up with some successful marketing ideas that had created my business. But did this success bring me my true strength?

I immediately went back to November 1986 when my father died and I just wanted to climb into that casket with him. I had my son to raise, and that is the only reason I didn't.

Or was this the reason? Who held me time and time again? I was so ill when I had my son, and I will never forget my doctor just sitting on my hospital bed holding my hand and saying, "I am doing everything I can." I had no clue. I just wanted to get well so I could take my son and go home. In those days, C-section patients and babies were kept six days minimum.

The nurse that came in on the seventh night who changed my fever-stricken night gown and my IVs smiled at me and said, "You will be okay in the morning."

That morning when my doctor came in, I knew I was okay. No fever, no pain, and I was in such a good mood. He looked at me and said, "What happened? Your fever is gone."

I told him that the red-haired midnight nurse told me that I was going to be okay when she changed my soaking gown and IVs. He just looked at me curiously. Didn't he know this red-haired nurse? Then he made me a promise. "If you can keep this fever down for the next twenty-four hours, you might be able to go home with your son."

Yes, I prayed and prayed a thankful prayer. I just kept thanking God for my sweet baby boy, and I promised him that if he healed me, I would be the best mom possible. Twenty-four hours later, I was discharged from the hospital with a full recovery from my drastic illness.

All the times I silently beat myself up for what I had done by leaving my reliable paycheck from the bank and opening my shop made me realize that God had been holding me in his ever-understanding and embracing arms.

This incredulous realization just swept over me, and I felt such a sudden peacefulness within me. It's hard to describe. I just know I felt this sudden burst of energy and well-being. Those grains of sand just hit me like a ton of rocks.

22

Prince Charming Arrives

If I hadn't had the shop, I would not have met the people that God put into my life. I would have never met Ron. Mother could not understand why I was not married to a wealthy Greek man and living in a big house and not having to work outside of the home. Sure, there were some around, but it didn't happen that way. I married a non-Greek, and it did not work out except that I had my son. I was content with my single life and deep down knew that if I would ever marry again, it sure wouldn't be another German!

My son, Stephen, was now in the military, and I was so alone. Burying myself in my business, I just kept working longer and longer hours. It was easy to live this kind of life.

Every once in a while, Mother would say, "Do you think your Prince Charming is going to come walking in that shop door? You need to go back to church. You need to get out. You need to do this, and you need to do that."

Sheesh. I was too darned tired to even think about going anywhere after I left my shop unless it was to run up to the local grocery store and get some supplies for the next day.

Monday through Friday, religiously at five o'clock in the morning, I would turn on the kitchen radio and tune into

WCER 900 AM. That's when the *Ron Riegler Show* would start. Ron had such a beautiful voice and was so much fun on the air. He played all of my favorites like Frank Sinatra, Dean Martin, and naturally, some Elvis and the Beatles too.

Frequently, he would talk about what he did over the weekend. Oftentimes, he would mention that he had taken his mother to an apple fair or some other event. *Hmm*, I wondered. *Is he single?* Then every so often, in the evening, he would have a live show spinning his records at a local theater. I used to think, maybe I could go out there and meet this gorgeous-voiced man. But of course, I didn't. I was too tired and just figured anybody with that beautiful of a voice just had to be married with ten kids or, the very least, have ten women after him.

The owner of this radio station, Jack, would stop into the shop when he was out cold calling in regard to radio advertising to the merchants on Main Street. He would walk into the shop; I would greet him with a cookie or brownie and say, "No!" We would both laugh because he knew he was not going to get an ad sale from me, and he also knew he would get his free treat.

Shortly after my first surgery, I was in the shop extremely depressed. I knew my surgeon would have a fit if he knew I was there. I was supposed to be in bed with my leg elevated due to my recent hospitalization. But I needed to be there to at least answer the phone and handle the writing up of the orders because my staff was busy trying to work in the kitchen and do my work.

There I was, seated behind my desk, with my leg propped up on two pillows fighting back my fears of not being able to pay my bills on time. Jack came in and at once walked over to me and asked, "What is going on with you?" I told him about my surgery and how I wasn't even supposed to be there.

He was truly sorry for what was happening to me and tried to reassure me that everything would be okay. I did not attempt to get up to offer him a free treat, and I knew he understood. We chatted for a while, and off he went to pursue his sales for the day.

The very next morning, I was in my kitchen trying to maneuver around using a walker and trying to get some baking done. It is not easy hopping on one foot, holding onto a walker, and trying to prepare cake batter and fill cake pans, let alone get those pans to the oven to bake. The worse part was when they were done baking. Removing the pans took strength because I was trying not to step on my leg and sure did not want to spill any cake layers on the floor. But I had to get these cakes baked because my decorators were due in at seven in the morning, and they had to be cooled and ready to be iced off and decorated.

As usual, at five, I hobbled over to my radio to turn it on. There was Ron starting his show, and after the first song played, I heard him say, "It's a beautiful day today with fleecy white clouds, just like your buttercream frosting, isn't it, Evie?" I couldn't believe it! Not only had I lost the ability to walk on both legs, but I was also losing my mind. That anesthetic had melted my brains.

Ron played another song, and after that one, he made another remark! "Hey Cookie Queen up in North Canton, how are you doing today?" Now I knew I was out of my mind. I just couldn't believe what I had heard. These kinds of cracks went on for the next few days. Jack must have told Ron about my depressed state of being. He probably also told him that I listened to his show every morning.

If Ron was trying to cheer me up, he was certainly doing it. Then one morning, I was sitting on the other side of the shop. I had told my employee that I had my leg propped up with pillows and that I did not want any customers to see me that way. I didn't want them to lose confidence that my shop would not perform our services for their preorders. It was bad enough I had turned down so many orders, let alone let people see me like that. I had my big mixing bowls, flour, salt, and shortening. I was making piecrust mix for future use. I was busy and not in any mood for any antics.

Around midmorning, a man entered, and my employee went over to him and said, "Welcome to Evie's. May I help you?"

I watched with curiosity as he said to her, "Are you Evie"?

She replied no, but she repeated her offer to help him.

Again, he persisted. "I want to speak to Evie."

Again, she tried to explain that she could take care of whatever he needed.

By now, I was getting ticked. Just who was this big guy anyways? I knew I had never seen him, but there was just something about him that made him seem so darned familiar. He didn't look like a salesman, and I had become quite an authority on salesmen cold calling me.

Then in a booming voice, he yelled across the room and asked, "Is that Evie over there?" Oh shoot, he had seen me, and what could I do? My poor employee just looked at me, and I gave her a look like, *Okay fine, I'll take care of this guy!* I could see he was one of those "I have to talk to the boss personally, you won't do" types.

I lowered my leg gently from my pillow pile, grabbed my walker, and hopped on one foot over to him. Keep in mind, my room was very wide, and this was quite a feat for me.

Just as snotty as I could, I said, "I'm Evie, may I help you?"
He smiled and said, "I talked to you this morning."

I replied, "Oh, no, you didn't. I've had lots of phone calls
this morning, and they have all been women. I did not talk
to you." Why did this man seem so familiar?

He smiled and said that it was a one-sided conversation.
That was a new one for me. I looked at him questioning his
answer. He again said, "I talked to you this morning. I talk
to you every morning. My name is Ron Riegler."

I just started laughing and laughing. I answered, "You're
right, you did talk to me this morning, and you do talk
to me every morning." I couldn't stop laughing, and my
employee stared at us both and tried to figure out what was
so funny. Obviously, she had never listened to his program.

I told Ron to come on over where I was trying to hide
from my customers and attempting to get some work done.
Slowly, I climbed back up on my stool and propped my leg
up on my pillows. It was easy to hide from my customers
with such a big man sitting next to me.

He was absolutely one of the smartest men I had ever
talked to. I must admit, his beautiful voice was captivating.
I had so much fun chatting with him. We visited for about
an hour, and then he said he had to get back to the station because the verdict was coming in on the OJ Trial. He
wanted to make sure their satellite was working correctly so
they could broadcast the news for their audience. After he
left, I was in such a good mood and could not believe the
joke that had been played on me.

The next morning, as my usual habit, I turned on my
radio. Well, Ron decided to have even more fun that morning. He kept referring to baking techniques, recipes, and so
on, and always saying, "Isn't that right, Evie?" Oh my gosh,
what would Jack think? I was so afraid he would be fired.

He kept this up for two weeks. Every day, he made little comments about me, my shop, my treats; it was endless. Even my customers heard these antics, and they called to let me know and wanted verification that indeed I was the one he was talking about. They really thought it was hysterical. I tried not to be flattered by all of this attention. Deep down, I was cracking up.

Finally, he called and asked me if I would like to go to a movie the next night. It was Saturday. Big deal. It just meant all the orders should be picked up at four in the afternoon, and I could go home earlier and crash.

I explained to him that I did not go out and that I put in long hours. He already knew those facts from Jack, but he explained that we could go to an early movie, and it would not be a late night for me.

I agreed to go out with him, but being the cautious type, I said he could pick me up at my shop rather than my apartment. Was my curiosity slanting my judgment? Maybe Mother was right. Maybe I needed to get out of the shop and have some fun.

However. I sensed that he was not in a good mood. Something had happened at the station. I was exhausted from an especially busy week, and I didn't even want to go out with him. I was just being polite and kept reminding myself that I instantly liked him at our first meeting.

After the movie, he brought me straight back to the shop. I had my van key in my lap. As soon as he stopped in front of my shop, I opened the door of his car with my key in hand and practically leaped out saying, "Thanks for the movie." I slammed his car door and got into my van.

I waited for him to pull out. I didn't want to take the chance of him following me home, so I just leered at him until he backed up his car and exited my parking lot. He peeled out, and I thought, *Great, he has a bad temper too. Beautiful voice, huh.* I was never going to tolerate a bad-tempered man again. What a horrible night. I was so disappointed and sorry, I had lost some valuable sleep due to this persistent man.

You just can't imagine what happened on Monday morning. As usual, I turned on my radio and started listening to his show. Now I knew this nutcake was going to get fired. But he would not let up, and what was so funny was the way he would lead into a song with a comment about me. Or he would end a song and make a comment about me.

I could have just died when he said, "I'm going to let Frank do my talking for me," and started Frank Sinatra's song, "I've Got a Crush on You, Baby Doll." Oh yes, once again, customers called my shop to verify that those cracks were about me. I had no idea so many people that I knew were up so early and listened to him every morning, just like me!

Another two weeks of this constant barrage of nonsense went on until I could not take it anymore. My employees were cracking up. They thought it was hilarious that Evie had an admirer. Admirer? This man was absolutely insane!

I called him at the radio station and told him he just had to stop his craziness because I feared Jack would fire him. He assured me Jack was having lots of fun with this too.

I kept thinking about our first meeting and how much I enjoyed talking to him. I must also confess how darned much fun it was listening to him go on and on every morning. So I got up the guts to ask him if he wanted to join me at my cousin's house on Sunday for dinner and to celebrate her son's birthday. Little did I realize that he figured, "Oh my, a Greek girl inviting me to be with the family…I must be in like flint!"

Well, he must have been on his best behavior. He had everyone in stitches and almost charmed my mother. It is time to let you know that Ron's father was German and his mother is Welsh. My poor mother was glad someone made me laugh, but why couldn't he be Greek and rich too?

From then on, Ron would pick me up on Saturday evenings, and we would go out. He was always mindful of the fact that I had had a busy day. He loved the theater, and so did I. I just wish I had met him years before. He loved good food, good times, and I was always too tired. He had so many interesting friends.

When we would arrive at our destination, Ron would nudge me to wake me up. I couldn't help myself. I would always fall asleep in the car on our way to whatever he had planned for that evening. He would politely ask if I was up to going inside. I would always beg for his forgiveness at doing it again. We would go in, and I tried to stay awake and be a good date. He would always whisper to me, "It's okay, we won't stay long."

My health just would not return to me. When Ron would finish at the station around one o'clock in the afternoon each day, he would call me to see if I needed errands or deliveries or anything else done. I soon learned to take him up on his offers.

A few days of me needing his help made him realize that he should come up every day after work and not call first. How did I ever get along without him? He ran all of the deliveries and always said to me when he came in, "So what supplies do you need picked up?"

Not only did he run for supplies, but upon return, he also promptly unloaded the van and put everything away for me too. There was the daily chore of writing invoices that needed to be mailed out for my corporate orders. An old bank saying was "If you don't get those bills out, the payments won't come in."

One day, Ron said to me, "You know, you really do need a computer." I just looked at him and said, "How much? I don't have the time nor the desire to work on one." He reassured me that he would take care of creating the invoices on this new piece of equipment. He advised me that he could justify the cost of this computer because he could make me cute sales signs and flyers. Now that was a secret desire of mine for some time. Instead of trying to get to the printer, Ron could do it for me.

Eventually, it became clear to Ron and to me that I needed him full-time, all the time, which left him no time for the radio station. He did leave the station, and now he was coming in at five every morning. He lived across town, which made it inconvenient for him; nevertheless, he was there every morning.

One morning, he wanted to know if I wanted to have a cup of coffee with him and a muffin. I told him, "Not right now, I'm busy. We can do that in a few minutes." He walked away and left me to my work.

About ten minutes later, there he was again with that same offer. I repeated my refusal. He walked away. There he was again pestering me. This went on for an hour.

Finally, I said, "Okay, let's have a cup of coffee and a muffin." We went over to our work stools, and he suddenly dropped to one knee in front of me. I looked down at him and wondered what the heck was his problem.

Then he said, "Will you marry me?"

"*What!*" I was so surprised and could not understand his question. "Ron, why do you want to get married?"

He very sweetly said, "Because I can't see myself living without you."

Oh no, my perfect friendship, and what would my mother think! I told him we needed to think this through. I had had my heart broken before and didn't need it smashed again.

He was so shaken. He just walked away with his head down and acted like a beaten-up little puppy. He would not talk to me for the next two weeks. He came to work every day but would not even look at me, let alone talk to me. Now I had the one-sided conversations.

I just couldn't bear it anymore. It was such a beautiful day in May. I went to him and said, "Would you like to drive up to Dogwood Park and see the blossoms?" He reluctantly agreed.

We walked through the park, admiring the blossoms, and he just started to tell me how much he loved me and how he did not want to be alone anymore. I tried to explain to him that I didn't need to be married. I was independent and was not about to relinquish this.

But as we walked, I also feared his loss. What if he walked away and I never saw him again? He was so serious and not about to accept my refusal. It was his way or the highway.

I gave him a hug and said, "All right." He had a ring box in his pocket and presented his ring to me. He admitted that he had placed this box in his pocket every day, hoping to present it to me. It was beautiful, and I scolded him for spending so much money on it. I slipped it onto my finger.

I asked him how he knew my ring size, and he just smiled. Those theater people.

We went to see my mother. I proudly showed her my ring and her immediate response was, "Give it back to him. Give it back to him." Mother was grief-stricken.

I knew I was in trouble. I tried to explain to her that I did not want to do that. I also explained to her that we would be setting a date in the near future. She said that she would not attend my wedding. I was saddened to hear that and just knew deep down that if my father had been present, he would have been happy for me.

When you have a grown married son that lives out of state that has his planned vacations and you own a business that has its established busiest times, how do you try to work around all of that to figure out a date for your wedding?

For several years, I had been closing the shop for two weeks after Christmas. I told Ron that would be the time to get married. That was fine with him. We were getting married. "You plan it honey, and I'll be there" was his attitude.

After Mother's chilly reception, I knew I had better call Stephen before the family did. His response was almost as frigid as Mother's. But he did agree he could come to the wedding and walk me down the aisle.

I was glad that our date would work for him. He did take this time as vacation, which I appreciated. December 25th was Christmas, December 26th was Ron's birthday, and I needed at least two days to recuperate from the holidays, so December 28th was chosen.

23

I Do (and He Did Too)

When you help plan other people's weddings and design cakes for everyone else, what do you do for yourself? I thought and thought and thought. I told Ron that music is what brought us together so that had to be the theme of our wedding.

I was Greek Orthodox, Ron's Methodist, and I did not even consider asking him to get married in my church. It was not necessary, but I did want a religious ceremony somehow.

Thanks to my dear niece, Stephanie, we were able to book the beautiful Congress Lake Clubhouse facility. Patrick, who was the catering manager, and I had worked on many parties before. When I called to tell him I needed to coordinate a wedding with him, and that it was mine, he was delighted. At last, somebody liked this idea.

There's a saying in the wedding business, "It starts with the ring." Next, you pick out the wedding/reception site and set your wedding date according to their available dates. Thank goodness, Patrick had my date open. I shared all my ideas with him, and he was so receptive to all of them.

If I had not owned my shop, I would not have been able to have the contacts nor the resources to create the wedding that we had. It was elegant, beautiful, and fun. Our guests, as well as Patrick, had never experienced what we did. Ron and I conceived a fun production.

Ron and I started our planning. Ron's background is not only as an actor and director in the theater, but he is a talented writer too. Years beforehand, he and his friend had an advertising agency.

One afternoon, Ron and I sat down together and designed our wedding invitations. He still had a source to order special paper, and he placed that order. Naturally, the paper was a light rose (my favorite color). Since we were getting married in the winter and I loved everything Victorian, Ron created the most memorable invitations. It had trailing musical notes and asked our guests to join us. There was a Victorian couple in a sleigh. We could hardly wait for our guests to receive and see them. They really were artistic. Ron even created return mailing labels with the same design.

Weeks before our date, Ron showed his friend Bob, who had a shop at his home, a design for our centerpieces. It was for an upright wooden musical clef on a round wooden stand. He also showed him a sample of an upright black musical note on a round stand to use as our table numbers. This woodworking whiz promised us he could easily make these for us.

Upon completion, Ron took them down to our friends Jo and Bob Brewster. They owned a downtown Canton family floral shop. The centerpieces and table numbers were decorated in metallic gold silk poinsettias. These items looked outstanding on our tables.

I had a pattern for a wooden Victorian sleigh placed in a dresser drawer for a "someday get it made by someone." Ron showed this to the whiz, and he promptly said, "Yes, I can make that for you too." We asked him if he could deliver it to the club early in the morning of our wedding day. He did, and it was placed next to the Christmas tree. It was so elegant. After the wedding, we surprised Bob by telling him to take the sleigh home. He was so delighted because while he was making it for us, his son kept wishing that it were his. Now he could take it to his son for a wonderful surprise.

After our ceremony, I was so surprised. We had put on our invitations that we did not want any gifts. But our friends did not listen. The sleigh was brimming with wedding gift packages. That big white sleigh next to the club's huge and beautifully decorated tree was outstanding.

I wanted a really different reception, so this is what we did. Ron and I loved the element of surprise. I had reserved seating. When our guests arrived, they were ushered into the front living room. I had a table with a white floor-length table covering, a white eyelet shorter-cover tablecloth, and the seating cards arranged in guest order. My cousin Joanne knew I loved angels and had given me the most beautiful white Victorian one. I had it on this table with a generous amount of artificial white snow. The table was a dream fantasy.

Our wedding reception started at nine o'clock on this Sunday morning. I was worried that some of our friends might not arrive on time. That worry was unfounded.

Patrick had servers greet our guests with offerings of apple juice and orange juice. They also had small squares of breakfast pizza. I had seen sausage and scrambled egg bite-sized pizzas in a magazine once and told Patrick about it. He agreed; that would be a different appetizer to serve. They were a huge hit!

The entrance doors to the library were closed as well as the large french doors to the main dining room. The guests were contained in the living room.

Ron was having lots of fun with everyone. They kept asking him where I was. He jokingly kept telling everyone that he had me bound up and gagged in another room. He was not taking any chances. They roared. I was hiding in the ladies powder room. I arrived in work clothes that morning and put on my wedding attire in this room.

There were several guests to whom we wanted to give appreciation gifts. Interestingly enough, the number of remembered guests equaled the number of tables. Therefore, one special guest was seated at a table.

Ron and I composed a note of appreciation to each of them. The envelope was addressed to the designated person, and the correct table number was inscribed in the bottom left portion of the envelope. The contents expressed our love and appreciation for them and our wish for them to take home the table's centerpiece.

Have you ever wondered what the hosts do with the centerpieces at a wedding? No one had to guess at our party. The guests were so surprised when they saw an envelope addressed to them with the offer to take home our piece. Besides, what would I have done with all of them?

Since our accent colors were silver and gold, I had purchased bags of shredded gold Mylar. I used these as fillers in plastic champagne glasses. We inserted a Snickers cookie on a stick, individually wrapped and bowed with gold ribbon into each glass. Patrick assured me that he would put one at each place setting for me and he did.

I also told him that I wanted to incorporate the color of metallic silver by using silver stars. I showed him a star with the middle cut out in a circle. Then I asked him if I could come in the day before to fold his white linen napkins accordion style and put them through the stars. "Oh, Evie, you just bring me those stars the day before, and I will fold the napkins and insert them into the stars. I will have them at each place setting. Do not worry about doing this yourself.

I assigned this task of cutting the middles out of the stars to Ron. I gave him many weeks notice because I'm the type that likes to work ahead, especially with our busy season, and I didn't want to be bogged down with last minute items the day before the wedding.

If you have never tried potato chips this way, you must. A good customer of mine years before had just returned from Chicago and could hardly wait to tell me about the newest food fad there. She told me how utterly scrumptious potato chips one-half dipped in chocolate are. Later on, I had done many for my son's wedding. I always told my customers about them too. The combination of salt and chocolate is very exciting to the taste buds. Just as this is with the chocolate on the Ritz, so are one-half dipped potato chips. This is an extremely time-consuming task but oh so worth it.

I warned Ron that the day before the wedding, I would be busy baking our wedding cake and cookies and that he could take care of dipping all of the chips for me.

I used the same heart-shaped dishes I had used for Stephen's wedding. Patrick set these out on each table for me too. Well, I kept reminding Ron that the stars needed done before the wedding, so the chips could be done the day before. That stack of uncut stars stayed in the same spot for two months. We were not on the same timeline.

I decided I wasn't going to go nutsy over this, so I ignored it. The day before the wedding, Ron started cutting 130 stars. At the end of the day, his hand was killing him. I had suggested that he cut a few every day so that his hand would not give him any pain, but he chose to do this chore his way.

Thank goodness, my adorable little niece, Erika, called me before Christmas and asked if she could help me with my wedding. I told her she could come to my shop the day before to help Ron dip the potato chips. She was thrilled. She remembered these and warned me that she might nibble more than she dipped.

She reported for chip-dipping duty early the morning before the wedding. Ron was off the hook. Erika dipped bags and bags of chips for us. After they dried on sheets of wax paper, she arranged them in all my heart-shaped dishes.

So many of our guests had rewarded Ron and me with so much love and kindness that we wanted to show them a remembrance. I knew all of them were chocoholics, so I baked chocolate pecan fudge pies for them. I put them in a box and tied them with pink tulle. On top of the box was an addressed envelope to the designated recipient along with their designated table number. Patrick put these boxes at the designated place settings. Judge Denny Clunk performed our ceremony and graciously stayed for our reception. We surprised him with one of these pies.

* * *

Chocolate Pecan Fudge Pie

The recipe calls for a chocolate crumb crust, but I always used my regular baked pie shell. I felt that using this chocolate crust would be too much chocolate even though I am a chocoholic.

Ingredients for chocolate crust

> 1 ¼ cups chocolate wafer crumbs
> 1/3-cup salted sweet cream butter or margarine melted

Directions
Combine the chocolate crumbs and the 1/3 cup of melted butter. Firmly press mixture on bottom and sides of a 9-inch tart or pie pan. Bake at 350 degrees for 6–8 minutes. Remove from oven to cool on a cooling rack. Prepare the filling.

Ingredients for filling

> 1/2 cup salted sweet cream butter or margarine (I always used Parkay or Imperial Margarine.)
> 3/4 cup firmly packed brown sugar
> 3 eggs
> 1 package semisweet chocolate morsels (12 ounce), melted
> 1 teaspoon vanilla extract
> 1/2 cup all-purpose flour
> 1 cup coarsely chopped pecans (walnuts could be substituted)

Directions

Cream 1/2 cup butter or margarine. Gradually add the brown sugar, beating at medium speed of an electric mixer until blended. Add eggs, one at a time, beating after each addition. Mix in the melted chocolate, vanilla extract, and flour. Stir in the pecans. Pour the mixture into the prepared crust. Bake at 375 degrees for 25 minutes (until a toothpick inserted in the middle comes out clean). Cool completely on a wire rack. Pie can be stored at room temperature.

Cooled pie can be garnished with whipped cream. If using any type of cream topping, pie should be stored in the refrigerator.

* * *

I did not garnish my pies because I gift-wrapped them in boxes to use as my appreciation gifts at the designated place settings.

A few days before the wedding, Ron drove up to the club and borrowed large dinner plates from Patrick. I used these for my cookie platters. That way, I did not have to worry about buying or renting cookie plates. I had also told Patrick that his employees could keep any leftover cookies. Ron predicted there would not be any leftovers on those platters. He was right.

The evening before our wedding, we took all the items that we needed for our day except for the cake. God bless Patrick, he verified our delivery the night before and said, "Just scratch these chores off your list."

May I state that if you are working with a caterer, make sure they help you with everything that needs done. The old adage, "Ask and ye shall receive," is quite appropriate for a wedding. Patrick had always been a delight before whenever I had coordinated my customer's parties with him. He outdid himself trying to please me with mine. It helped that he loved all of my ideas too.

On the morning of the wedding, Ron and I arrived at seven o'clock to set up the wedding cake along with my decorator Cary. I need to describe our cake. I surely didn't have the time to bake cake from scratch, and that was fine with us both because we both loved Betty Crocker's dark chocolate cake and Pillsbury's red raspberry. When you can't decide what flavors to make, you make them all. In our case, I stuck to these two flavors. If this had been a customers order, I would have suggested having multiple flavors showcased in each tier. Keep in mind, I was trying to regain my strength from Christmas and to get married too. Each tier consisted of one layer of chocolate and one layer of red raspberry with chocolate walnut buttercream between the layers. As far as I knew, none of our guests were allergic to chocolate or walnuts.

Since pink is my favorite color, music was our theme, and we both loved chocolate, combining these loves was the deciding factors for my design. Remembering what I always talked to my brides about—I needed to keep Ron's height in mind. We had about 120 guests, which translated to not many big cake tier sizes.

It was more important to me to have a big-enough display so Ron would not look overbearing at the cake table. I had already instructed Patrick that there would be plenty of leftover cake and to distribute it to the employees.

All of the tiers were iced off in chocolate buttercream. Then I had Cary run cascading floral stems in this same frosting. She made small musical notes in chocolate along these stems. At the rounded part of the note, she attached a red raspberry buttercream pink rose. On the tops of the tiers, Cary filled in with beautiful pink red raspberry buttercream roses with chocolate frosting leaves.

I knew the round cake table size at the club, and I knew the layout I wanted to incorporate, so this is what I did. Years beforehand, Mother had given me a seraphim angel named Evangeline. One of my employees one Christmas also gave me one named Iris. They were colored mostly in pink.

Patrick provided a floor-length white tablecloth for the cake table. I used a white lace one as the overlay cloth. I brought lots of pink tulle to create the illusion of pink clouds. I had Wilton clear plastic plates and tall pillars. I really did prefer stacked tiers with no separation, but again, I had to take into consideration Ron's stature.

Cary and I arranged the decorated tiers on the pillars. We left the top smallest tier smooth with no decorations. For my floral bouquet, I was carrying a large white orchid. After our ceremony, it was placed on top of this tier.

I puffed yards and yards of the pink tulle around and up the tiers. Then I arranged the seraphim angels and two other Victorian ones that I had in the tulle. It really did look like a bit of heaven.

As Cary and I worked on the cake table, Jo and Bob Brewster, our dear floral friends, were there early too to decorate the library for us. I did not even look at what they were doing. I was busy at the cake table. Then I checked all the tables to make sure Patrick had set out all my items as promised. He had followed my instructions to perfection.

Now let me explain to you what the Brewsters did. They arrived with yards and yards of white tulle, white silk poinsettias, and a plentiful array of iridescent gold silks. Inside of the library was a plain wall. They fashioned a draping arch out of the tulle. They decorated it with all the bountiful decorations they brought. I never saw this area until I marched down the aisle. I was absolutely delighted. After our reception, we took pictures in front of this area, and the decorations showed so beautifully.

Patrick had instructed his employees, per Ron's request, to set up white wooden folding chairs theater style in this room. It was a large room, and they arranged a generously sized center aisle for Stephen and me to walk down.

We had allowed for about thirty minutes of appetizers and juice to be passed out to the guests. Then Ron instructed Jack, our cupid ambassador, to introduce himself to the gathered audience. Jack explained to the crowd that he had sent Ron up to my shop to try and cheer me up and that he had hoped today would happen. Then Jack read a love poem that Ron had written and given to me our first Valentine's Day.

As soon as Jack finished, Fred, our DJ, played "Goin' to the Chapel and We're Gonna Get Married." As the song played, Jack told people to go in and be seated. As you can imagine, the guests cracked up.

Stephen came back to the powder room to get me and take me down the aisle. He was pleasantly surprised when he saw me in my light pink Victorian gown and pink tulle hat. My gown had roses and pearls and was more than I dreamed of having, but my dear Doreen insisted that I have this gown for my wedding. She had worked out a special price just for me. Now you see what I mean about all my dear friends that I had.

Walking over to the library, I saw the white wooden sleigh overflowing with gifts. We had stated on our invitations that their presence with us on our day was the only presents we wanted. We had not wanted anyone to bring us anything.

As Stephen and I walked down the aisle, Freddie played "You Light Up My Life." Ron was facing Judge Clunk and the tulle arch. As the music started to play, he turned around to sneak a peak at me walking down with Stephen. I was beaming, and the look on his face was priceless. His jaw had dropped, and he looked faint. I stood next to him, and he just glowed. He had written some of our vows, and I could tell Judge Clunk liked our ceremony.

After the ceremony, Judge Clunk instructed Ron to give me a kiss, which he did. We walked down the aisle and beamed at our guests. Melanie instructed everyone to exit the library through the bar where they were each given a glass of non-alcoholic champagne. Then she told everyone to gather around the wedding cake table to join the bride and groom in a toast. Now I have to tell you about our dear friend Melanie. She is such a talented singer and loves to perform at weddings. We had asked her to be our wedding coordinator, so to speak, just to make sure everything went according to our wishes. If you cannot hire a professional wedding coordinator to help you on your wedding day, then you must enlist the help of a good friend. I sure hope you have one like Melanie. She met us at our cake table. She handed us our champagne glasses (which of course the Brewsters had decorated in silks for us) and poured our champagne into our glasses. She gave the most delightful toast. Ron said some very endearing words to me. Then I spoke, "Today, I have married my best friend, someone who knows my past, believes in my future, and accepts me for just the way I am." Years before I had seen this somewhere and never forgot it. It sure described our relationship. Our love truly had been based first on friendship.

Patrick went over to the one set of french doors, and Melanie went to the other set. They opened the doors and Melanie in her boisterous voice announced "please enter the dining room, go to your numbered table and you will be served your brunch".

As stated before, Patrick was receptive to my ideas. My friend Stephanie had given me this recipe years before for a fresh sliced tomato, basil leaves, and thin slices of mozzarella cheese woven in a basket weave design. A light basil pesto dressing was drizzled over the top of this plated creation. These were served with our sandwiches.

Since this was a brunch, I asked the chef to make us ham and gruyère cheese monte christo sandwiches (ham and cheese sandwich that is dipped in egg, then fried like french toast and lightly sprinkled with powdered sugar on top). Patrick suggested we serve small pitchers of maple syrup to each table too. The guests were delighted with the salad and sandwiches. They were good surprises for them. As soon as the guests had finished their light lunch, their plates were removed and a generous assorted platter of cookies was taken to each table. Slices of cake were delivered as well. The guests were now on their second and third cups of coffee and tea.

Always cut the cake before your meal, that way it is served as your dessert. Oftentimes guests have to leave before they have been able to have any cake. I have been to receptions where hours seem to go by before the cake is cut and served and then the bride's family complains that there was leftover cake. Get it cut and served.

Ron summoned Melanie and told her that we were going back to the library with our family so Penny, a family friend, could take pictures in front of our bridal arch. As we left the room, Melanie sang a cappella the "Lord's Prayer" in her beautiful soprano voice. It was such a tender exit. After our pictures were taken, we went over to our sleigh. We were told by my family to open our gifts so the family could view the beautiful array. As I said before, we were just overwhelmed with everyone's generosity.

While Stephen and Ron loaded our gifts into our van, I went back to the powder/rest room to take off my beautiful gown and hat. I changed back into my work clothes and gathered up all my items. Dressing at the church/reception site is such a good idea. You don't have to worry about getting your gown wrinkled in the car.

Ron helped me with my apparel, and Stephen accompanied us back to our apartment to help us unload everything. We gave hugs and said good-bye to him and our daughter-in-law, Christine, and started our adventure to Disney World for our honeymoon.

24

What a Wonderful Way to End the Year

I had been to Florida before but had always flown. Dummy me, I guess I just did not realize how long of a drive it was. I was so glad when Ron surprised me by saying after we got into West Virginia that we should stay there overnight. We checked into a lovely hotel, ate dinner, and then we drove over to the Festival of Lights, located at Oglebay Resort in Wheeling, West Virginia.

It was such a beautiful, clear evening, and I was so thrilled. I had heard about this winter wonderland on Oglebay's golf course but had not even imagined what I would be seeing. If you ever get the chance, please drive through here during the holidays. It is so worthwhile.

By the time we got back to the hotel, I didn't know if I could get out of the car. I had no idea how exhausted I had become. Ron, being the tender-hearted person that he is, helped me to our room and I knew I just had to collapse into bed.

The next morning, Ron was watching the weather report on TV, and I saw the announcement that there was a terrible winter storm coming. I asked Ron if that would be affecting us, and he assured me that this storm was headed a different way.

After breakfast, we loaded up the car and left for our adventure in Florida. I fell asleep and woke up when we were in the mountains of West Virginia. It looked like one of those little snow globes, and this globe had been turned upside down.

"Oh my gosh, Ron, is that the storm they were talking about this morning on TV?"

Ron admitted to me that it was. I had never driven through these mountains before let alone in a winter blast like this one. Ron assured me that it would be okay, but I was scared to death. I did not fall asleep again because I knew I had to stay awake as if this would have prevented us from sliding into a mountain.

I did not want to complain, but those hours of sitting was starting to really affect my leg. I had brought my pain pills along with me just in case, and bottles of water were in the back seat. Ron reached into the back seat to get these items for me. I needed a pill; I could not put it off any longer.

This storm was the storm of storms. I thought that once we got out of those mountains in West Virginia we would be all right. That snow just would not stop. There was even snow in North Carolina. We were stranded for hours along the highway. We saw dogs exiting their vehicles and running up the hills having such a good time. Adults and children were out along the side of the highways throwing snowballs at each other. People were even making snow people.

Not me. I was huddled with fright in my front seat of my van. I kept thinking how lucky we were in my new Windstar. There were so many vans, cars, and trucks that had slid into each other and into the side of the highway. I told Ron that it looked like some kind of war zone. Ron had been counting the accidents and told me that he had seen seventeen vehicles off the road, most of them upside down. I had never seen anything like this before, nor did I ever want to experience this again.

I didn't know if I should be mad at him or what. He had lied to me. I knew he just wanted us to go to Florida, but to head deliberately into a mess like this was unforgivable. We still talk about this crazy storm, and I'm not sure how we got through it. The grace of God was how we got through it!

Ron had counted on me sleeping through all of this. Well, I surprised him due to my fright. We laugh about this now. What an experience; it has given us something to talk about all of these years.

What I am sad about is how I felt in Florida. The weather was so perfect. But I was in such pain. Walking through Epcot was so enchanting. Ron had never been there before. But hours and hours, even taking rest breaks, still took its toll. Coming home, I just did not know how I was going to cope with my pain.

25

It Was Unexpected and Unwanted, but Unavoidable

I had never counted on bad health.

Of all the problems of personnel and capital and time schedules and suppliers and a thousand other problems any businessperson must deal with, I never counted on bad health. I had not counted on my legs giving out on me.

I had a history of problems with my legs swelling. When I worked as a teller at the bank, after I had stood all day, my legs would give me considerable pain. But when I went home and got a good night's sleep, they were back to normal in the morning. I had so much on my mind when I opened my shop that I never worried about my legs. As a matter of course, I always wore support hosiery and good support type walking shoes. That awful swelling did not happen when I worked in my shop. I was so happy toiling away on all my creations and perhaps I didn't notice the building discomfort.

I didn't realize that standing sixteen to eighteen hours a day would finally take its toll on me. One morning, as I was putting on my hose, I felt a small wet spot on my ankle. I just figured I hadn't toweled off properly and went back into the bathroom and wiped my ankle again with my bath towel. I put the incident aside and thought no more about it; I went over to my shop and put in my standard busy day.

That night, when I took off my hosiery, I felt another wet spot at my ankle. I couldn't understand what that was all about. I went into the bathroom to wash my hose and looked at my ankle. I didn't see anything unusual other than a slight wetness. I searched in the medicine cabinet and found a big gauze pad and some tape. I applied it to my ankle and collapsed into bed.

The next morning, before my shower, I checked this spot, and the gauze was all wet. Still not thinking much about it, after I showered, I applied another patch, a much heavier one, dressed, and went to the shop. It just never entered my mind that this was a problem. I could not remember ever scratching this area, so why was this seepage happening? I am not a diabetic and never have been. But my body was acting as though I was. I came to learn that this was an ulcer.

I don't know exactly how long this went on before the horrific pain started. Meanwhile, Joy, my dear older sister in Las Vegas, was battling breast cancer, and I used to scold myself. *You think you're in pain? You big wimp. Think about your sweet sister and what she's going through.*

Finally, the pain reached and passed the unbearable level. I called my doctor, who was also a customer at the shop. I guess that's why I was able to get in to see him so quickly. He asked a couple of questions, like if I had bumped my ankle. I just replied that I had no idea what was going on. He gave me a prescription for pain medication. I don't think he knew exactly what he was dealing with, but

I was in no mood to quibble. I flew out of his office and headed straight to the drug store to get my pain pills.

More pain was followed by more prescriptions. Each time, I was told that I needed to prop my leg up and to cut back on my working hours. How? I had worked like crazy to build my business, but with the increased business had come increased overhead. This meant more hard work to always pay my bills on time. Good news: the orders poured in. Bad news: the pain would not stop.

One night I just cried and cried. I finally told Ron that he needed to get me to the emergency room. He carried me to the car and carried me into the emergency room. The ER doctor looked at my ankle and immediately ordered the nurse to start an IV of morphine.

Now I understand how junkies can get hooked. After the first bag, the very kind nurse said, "Honey, I'm going to get you a little bit more. I don't know how you have been working with that ankle the way it is." Oh, the world was so wonderful and everything was beautiful, and I felt marvelous!

The ER doctor said I had to see my doctor the next day. He said I absolutely could not be on this leg and I had to be in bed. He had never seen such a large untreated ulcer as the one I had. Untreated ulcer? That's the first I heard of that. But that wonderful ER doctor knew exactly what he was doing. The next morning, Ron called the help, and I'll never forget my cross-trained loyal employees. They took care of everything.

Ron took me to my doctor. He said I had to remain on bed rest and it was vital that I choose from a list of three specialists he presented. I chose the plastic surgeon that the doctors chose when they need a plastic surgeon. I had heard of his excellent reputation. Fortunately, I was able to see him the next morning.

God bless Dr. Shaw and his miraculous hands. He was astounded when he saw my ankle's condition. I had to have a week of continuous bed rest and special localized treatment to get well enough to have my plastic surgery.

In the hospital after my surgery, I did not need pain medication. Dr. Shaw had performed a miracle on my leg. I could not believe that all the suffering was gone!

As I was trying to control my worries about the shop, my sister lost her battle with breast cancer. I was distraught because I was not permitted out of bed to fly out for her funeral. Grief is as terrible a wound to your heart and soul as surgery is to the treatment of an open ulcer on your ankle. I faced an incredibly difficult recuperation process.

I was off work a total of six weeks with complete bed rest before and after surgery. Then I was warned to only work one or two hours a day when I returned to the shop. And I did just that for the first few days. I had terrific help, and Ron had run things to the best of his ability with my coaching, but we were losing control of the business.

There were so many orders, and I wasn't there to take care of things. I had instructed my staff to turn down any additional orders and just take care of what we already had. That was a good idea, but their overtime killed me. So payroll and my expenses demanded the additional orders be undertaken at once.

Soon, I was back to my old habit of working long hours. After several months of this, the pain started again, and I knew I was in trouble. I certainly didn't want to go back to all the prior pain medication, especially since I had been warned about potential liver damage.

When the pain became unbearable, I reluctantly made my appointment and sheepishly faced Dr. Shaw. He examined me and said, "What happened to my surgery?" He shook his head. "You've been working long hours again, haven't you? Well, you have lost 60 percent of the skin graft I put on for you. I don't think I could ever do another surgery on this ankle again. You are facing serious consequences if you don't stop working the long hours."

I did cut back on my hours and on the orders. I had a lot of customers that argued with me, but I just explained that I couldn't take on any more. There are certain types of people who refuse to take no for an answer. And so for months, this is what I did until finally I knew that I could not pull it off anymore. Sometimes, just being on my leg for half an hour brought on that awful and all-too-familiar pain.

Ron and I reluctantly set up a plan to try to sell the shop. We had at least five very good prospective buyers. In my efficient banking style, I showed them my records of the repeat holiday corporate orders and assured them that these orders would be theirs.

I showed them my procedure books and other recipes. I showed them my drawings and designs for wedding cakes. I told them that all of the above was included in the sale along with all the advance orders, equipment, fixtures, and especially my reputation, and excellent name.

Then every one of my prospects said exactly the same thing, "You do all of this?" Well, of course I do all of this! That's why I'm Evie! The truth that I had dreaded with each of the prospective buyers came out at that moment. No one would commit to the amount of work that I had been doing for thirteen years. Unfortunately, that work is essential to achieving success. All of them gave me the same excuse about my personalized business. "If you're not here, they won't come in" was their common excuse not to buy my shop.

I had to face some very daunting facts. I had no buyers, and I had many wedding cakes ordered. I couldn't let my brides down, but what could I do? Now my health was at stake.

It was always my procedure to secure a wedding cake order with a 50 percent down payment to save that date. When I had so many orders for that date, I did not accept anymore. I was always booked solid a year in advance. That's what I had worked for! So Ron composed the most beautiful letter explaining that I was ill and had to close the shop. I enclosed their full refund check in with the letter and cried when he took them to the post office.

I accepted no orders for December. I accepted no cake orders for November. I just explained to all the callers that I could not accept any more orders, and all of them apologized and said they should have called in July. I didn't want anybody upset about anything.

I needed the cash from the Thanksgiving sales to pull off some current and future expenses that had to be met. My medical bills were unreal. I provided my employees and myself the very best hospitalization that money could buy, but there were still huge out-of-pocket expenses.

Thanksgiving was very busy, and my customers did not realize that this was the last holiday for my shop and that I would be closing that weekend. As the customers came in to pick up their orders, I told them that I was closing. There was a lot of crying, but somehow I got through that day with my leg killing me the whole time. The pain in my leg was nothing compared to the agony in my heart.

Thanksgiving weekend, Ron and I went over to the shop and thoroughly cleaned, which was not difficult because my shop was always exceptionally clean.

I had so much to do those last few days—what to keep, what to leave for the next tenant; and if I tried to sell, I probably wouldn't get that much anyhow. All of my equipment, pans, and so on were in such good condition. I was always so careful to keep everything so immaculate.

One of my friends at the bank knew of a lady that had worked out of her home for eighteen years baking. She wished she could have a storefront, so she moved into my spot when I closed.

26

Reflections

I kept thinking about the days when I first opened my shop and especially thought about my son, Stephen.

At the time, I didn't realize what it must have been like for him to be approaching his teen years and all that he had to deal with let alone with a mother that decided to go into business for herself and put in so many hours.

I was the baseball mom, the one that made sure lots of flowers were sold for the annual flower sale. I was the mom that always attended the school conferences, open houses, plays, and concerts. I was so committed to my shop that I sloughed off the open houses and other events. Stephen said he didn't mind, but I think he did. He was so used to my support.

As I looked around my pretty shop that had created so many customers—friends for me—I thought about Pop and knew that he liked this bigger location and all of the items I had made.

I started to reflect on the early days at my first place and so many things that had happened especially with my son. One time when he came in from school, I informed him that we were having a quick dinner and I had to get back to work. I had an early-morning pickup of apple dumplings, which meant that I would be working late.

Stephen looked at me and said, "I can help you make the dumplings, Mom."

I laughed and said, "You know, I tried to teach you to roll out piecrust dough as well as cut out cookie dough, but you have always refused, so how do you think you are going to help me?"

He grinned and replied, "You're right, I don't know how to roll out the dough, but I know how to put them together…you just roll out, and I'll assemble."

"Now how could you know how to do that?" I responded.

Stephen laughed. "Because I watch what you do and that's how I know how."

The old saying "seeing is believing" is so true. After dinner, I started rolling out, and Stephen set up our assembly line. I passed the seven-inch squares of dough over to his workstation. He immediately took a prepared apple, filled it with the cinnamon-and-raisin mixture and quickly brought the dough up into the corners.

Then he said, "Mom, pass me the cutout leaves of dough too. I know how to attach them to the tops like you do. Are we coloring the leaves green with egg yolk mixed with food coloring? I can use the small paint brush and apply the green carefully. Want to watch me?"

I was absolutely surprised. Stephen worked so quickly and knew exactly how to assemble and decorate the dumplings. "Stephen, when did you watch me?"

"Oh, Mom, you are always so busy working you don't notice me watching what you do."

I remembered those words with such a tug. Because I was so busy working, I didn't even know my son was there with me.

The good thing about living upstairs and having a shop downstairs is you don't have to worry about your child sleeping and you being at work. That's why my first shop had worked so well for me. I knew I would be working long hours and, I sure didn't want my child home alone while I was off in a strip center somewhere working.

So many times, I have suffered such guilt feelings that I could have been a better mother, have given him more time. The years went by so quickly, and then he was off to the Air Force at my insistence so that he could get his college education and not be burdened with student loans.

Stephen was so fast with his hands, especially when I would ask him to fold pie boxes. He would always ask, "How many?" I would always give him the same answer, "Just start folding. I'll let you know when you're done."

A short time later, he would report back to let me know how many he had folded, while secretly wishing that I would tell him that he was finished. Stephen would repeatedly ask, "How many more?" I stubbornly would insist that he needed to just keep folding.

After he had reached at least seventy-five, I would then tell him that he could finish tomorrow with another fifty. I always sold at least 125 pies for Thanksgiving along with all the cookie and cake orders. For some reason, that number never seemed to change.

The following year, when I needed pie boxes folded, somehow, Stephen did not remember how many he had folded for me the year before, so we had the same conversation: "How many do I have to do?" Oh, how I ached for those words when he was grown and gone.

It was also his question when I asked him to make chocolate on the Ritz. My sister's friend gave this novel item to her. She brought me a sample to try. I never realized how deliciously different a salt, chocolate, and peanut butter combination could be. I knew I just had to start selling these, and they would be a great addition to my cookie platters. These were such a hit, and I am forever grateful to whomever figured this one out. I am so sorry that I do not know who started this. I do know that my nephew at Waggoner Chocolates is selling a ton of these.

This was a great delight that Stephen could make too. He sure loved to devour them, but making them? Of course, all I had to do was show him once, and he had the process down perfectly. And of course we had that conversation of "how many do I have to do" all of the time.

* * *

Stephen's Chocolate on the Ritz

Ingredients

> 1 box of Ritz crackers
> 1 jar of Jif Peanut Butter
> dipping chocolate
> ample wax paper and a wire rack

Directions

Make peanut butter sandwiches with the crackers. Here's the clever part: If you put too much peanut butter between the crackers, the sandwiches will slide when you dip them. If you do not put enough in, then they won't have enough of the peanut butter taste.

Dip the assembled sandwiches in melted dipping chocolate and place on waxed paper to set up. I always placed sheets of waxed paper on my racks, and when we were done dipping, the filled racks were moved to a table to dry or set up. It's easier to use a rack or a cookie sheet if you have to move your items around.

If desired, colored sugar or crystals can be sprinkled on top.

After they dry, they can be placed in airtight containers. They are wonderful gifted in a decorative tin.

* * *

I used to have my customers drop off their tins, and I would fill them with chocolate on the Ritz. They used to have the best time giving these to their friends because they knew their friends could not guess what this cookie was. Once again, I did not have to incur the cost of buying tins. My customers were happy to provide them. They were perfect on my assorted cookie platters as well as bagging and bowing to place in my baskets. Dipped cookies just seemed to add that extra pizzazz.

They were such a hit, and it was a natural for Stephen to make for me. Once again, the "how many" questions were asked, and I would just reply, "Start making them, and I'll let you know when you're finished." Approximately, every half an hour or so, he would repeat his question.

After about an hour of him working, I would inform him that he was done but that I needed his help the next day after school. God bless my son. Sometimes, he would pitch in willingly, and on a few occasions, he would not, but I could never get over how darned quick he was and knew precisely how to do whatever I asked of him. You just had to show Stephen once, and that was it.

I remember the first time he came to me and said, "You're tired and have to get up early tomorrow morning. Just tell me the cookies you need to make tomorrow. I know how to make all your recipes, put the dough in your plastic containers, label, and place them in the refrigerator the way you want it done." My procedure book had not been conceived yet, but Stephen knew how to read a recipe and just did it.

Once again, I voiced my favorite line, "But how do you know how to do this?" With his big grin, he would give me the same answer, "Mom, I've watched you and how you do it. I know how."

He would send me off to bed, and when I would go down to the shop the next morning; he would have a carafe filled with coffee and a note that detailed what I would find in the refrigerator. The note always wished me a good morning and was always signed, "Love, Stephen."

I haven't told you about the cheesecakes that Stephen can make. Back then, he baked the ones that I offered my customers. Once again, I asked, "How do you know?" He always gave me the same answer. "Oh, Mom, I know how you do it."

Many times, he would send me off up the stairs, and he would stay up baking my cheesecakes for me. While they were in the oven, he would sit out in the living room doing his homework. My son now creates cheesecakes that are simply out of this world for his business friends. When there is a birthday in his office, the cheesecake requests come into Stephen for one of his creations.

Yes, I had hoped that Stephen would return home after his military stint, but it didn't work out that way. Yes, it would have been great for me. I always thought about different ways to expand the business but knew that I could not do it myself even though I had the very best employees.

Today, Stephen has a terrific job with the University of Wisconsin. He has authored his own books on website optimization, and I really do think he gets his big smarts from his grandfathers. He gets his hard-work ethics from them too. Stephen never complained about what time was dinnertime because I discovered quite early when I went to sell some brownies that he was satisfying his after-school hunger pangs quite nicely. I always tried to make sure that I had ample pans of brownies on the counter so when Stephen came home he could help himself.

The only time I really got mad at him was when I forgot to tag some pans that were sold and he swiped them. I really couldn't blame him because they were the best brownies ever.

I tried many, many brownie recipes. They were good, but I knew that somewhere there existed a brownie recipe that was *great*! I just hadn't found it yet. Just like Mom and my sister Joy, I always enjoyed trying new recipes.

Then one day at the grocery store, I saw a big display for Choco Bake, a new chocolate baking product. I looked at the description of the product on the box and marveled at what I was reading: No need to melt squares of chocolate for baking your chocolate recipes. Just squeeze the chocolate out of the premeasured one-ounce packets. What an ease and convenience! I looked on the back of the box, and there was a brownie recipe. I wondered if it was the recipe I had been searching for. It sounded so good that I bought a box and vowed to try this new recipe the first thing the next morning.

I did. And let me tell you, while they were cooling, the aroma of chocolate-filled every corner of the shop. I had made two pans and was just in the process of lightly sifting some powdered sugar on the first pan when my friend Bernie popped in. "Aah, brownies!" he said. "But what are you doing, Evie?"

"I'm trying a new recipe, and I'm doing what it says. I'm supposed to lightly dust the cooled pan with powdered sugar," I told him.

"Stop. Spread your chocolate buttercream frosting on that other pan."

"Okay." I did, and Bernie was right. I told him to come back later when the frosting was set up. He told me I could count on it.

When Stephen got home from school, I told him I had a special job for him. He rolled his eyes and told me he had a lot of homework to get started on.

I took him over to the counter and showed him the pans of brownies. "I need a worker with your special talents," I said. "This is a new recipe, and I need you to taste test them for me."

He swiped both pans and ran up the steps. A moment later, he returned and said, "Mom, these are fabulous. But I like the ones with the frosting better." He helped himself to a gallon of milk and disappeared back upstairs. It's a good thing Bernie never made it back that afternoon because Stephen polished them off.

Now I knew I had found the best brownies *ever*. Would you believe, for some reason or not, this recipe is not on the back of the box anymore? So here it is, and I hope Nestle Corporation is glad I am telling you about it.

We always made a quadruple batch, which used the entire box. This made four eight-inch square pans. I always cut the pan into thirds, which gave a yield of nine nice-sized pieces. These brownies were great on my cookie platters too. Platter size was the squares cut into one-half or quarters, then placed in paper baking cups. The small one-fourth size really made deliciously cute accents tucked into and on top of the other cookies.

This is the recipe for a single batch.

* * *

Best Brownies Ever

Ingredients

2 packets of Choco Bake
1/2 cup salted sweet cream butter, or 1 stick
2 eggs
1 1/4 cups sugar
1 teaspoon vanilla
3/4 cup flour and 1/8 cup flour.

Direction

The recipe indicated that the eight-inch square pan should be greased then lined with foil. I had seen that before in recipes, so I did this. The next batch I tried, I just sprayed my pan with cooking spray. Well, from then on, I just used the cooking spray, and they turned out just fine.

These are great with a sprinkling of powdered sugar, but I always frosted them off with my chocolate buttercream frosting. These are really good with maraschino cherry frosting too. (See buttercream frosting recipe chapter 4. Substitute the juice from a bottle of maraschino cherries for milk.) You can get creative and swirl peanut butter through the chocolate buttercream frosting too.

You can add nuts to the batter or chocolate chips. I never did. I always worried about customers that could not tolerate nuts in their diet.

I figured this one out myself. First, you need to hold the packets of Choco Bake under hot running water. Wipe the packets dry, then cut off the tops with a scissor. Squeeze from bottom down and out into a 1 1/2 quart–sized saucepan. Add the stick of butter. I always use a wooden spoon. On the stove top with a medium heat, melt the butter and Choco Bake stirring until mixed. *Do not boil.* Set this pan aside.

Place the two eggs in a small mixing bowl. Add the vanilla and beat. Set this aside.

When the saucepan mixture has almost cooled, add the egg mixture and stir until combined. Add the sugar and mix thoroughly. Next, add the flour and stir until well mixed.

If you want to add nuts, this can be done now.

Use a rubber spatula and scoop the batter into the prepared eight-inch square pan.

Bake in a 350-degree oven for about 20 minutes.

Brownies are like cheesecakes. It is difficult to tell when they have baked long enough. Too long, and they are overdone. Not long enough, and you have a gooey mess.

Here are the signs I looked for:

- The sides were slightly drawn inward.
- They looked evenly baked.
- When touched lightly with a fingertip, the batter would spring back.

Remove from oven and place on a wire rack to cool. Frost, allow the frosting to set up, and then enjoy!

27

Go Ye Now in Peace

This is the song by Joyce Elaine Eilers that I hum to myself every morning while I drive to my office. It's a song my church choir sings periodically after our Sunday morning liturgy before the congregation leaves. In these words I find an inner peace.

Go ye now in peace,
and know that the love of God will guide you.
Feel his presence here beside you
showing you the way.
In your time of trouble, when hurt and
despair are there to grieve you,
Know that the Lord will never leave you.
He will bring you courage.
Know that the God who sent his
Son to die that you might live,
Will never leave you lost and
alone in His beloved world.
Go ye now in peace. Go ye now in peace.

CPSIA information can be obtained at www.ICGtesting.com
Printed in the USA
LVOW10s0600160916

504808LV00019B/79/P

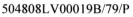

9 781680 283280